# contents

**PUTTING DOWN STONES** • *A Faithful Response to Urban Violence*

**INTRODUCTION**...............................................................2

**STUDY SESSION 1**
**The Spirit of Violence in Our Society**

Street Blessing ...............................................................5
*When violence comes home.*     *by* JIM WALLIS

Resisting Death Incarnate .......................................6
*The principalities of urban violence.*
        *by* BILL WYLIE-KELLERMANN

'Take Your Inheritance' .......................................10
*The challenge before the churches.*  *by* EUGENE F. RIVERS III

Behold the Nonviolent One ..................................11
*A peacemaking journey through the beatitudes.*
        *by* MARY LOU KOWNACKI, O.S.B.

Worth Fighting For ...........................................14
*The churches mobilize to save urban America.*
        *by* JIM WALLIS

**STUDY SESSION 2**
**Signs of Hope**

Sanctuary Is More Than Architecture................................17
*The church as safe place.*     *by* YVONNE DELK

In Jesus' Name.......................................................19
*Azusa Christian Community reclaims the poor
and dispossessed in Boston.*     *by* ANTHONY A. PARKER

Being Church in The 'Hood .............................................23
*Developing "Young Men With a Future."*
        *by* ELIZABETH PERPENER

A Time to Heal, A Time to Build......................................26
*Lessons from the Gang Summit.*     *by* JIM WALLIS

**STUDY SESSION 3**
**Confronting the Violence in Our Souls**

Out of the Hog Pen and Into Community .........................30
*Finding ourselves at last.*     *by* MAC CHARLES JONES

Our Common Hope...........................................................32
*Healing the violence in our souls and in society.*
        *by* ALEXIE M. TORRES

To Greet Brothers Without Fear.........................................34
*The long process of healing after rape.*    *by* JUDITH FLOYD

No Sympathy Required.........................................................36
*Why I live in the city.*     *by* KAREN LATTEA

The High Standards of Nonviolence...................................37
*Strategies for self-defense.*
        *An interview with* MARTHA J. LANGELAN

**STUDY SESSION 4**
**Rebuilding the Broken Walls**

'The Things That Make For Peace' ....................................40
*Churches in solidarity with street youth.*    *by* JEAN SINDAB

Creating Viable Options ......................................................41
        *by* AARON GALLEGOS

A Call to Action...................................................................43
*A 10-point plan to mobilize churches.*
        *by* THE TEN POINT COALITION

'We're in the Forgiving Business' ......................................44
*Barrios Unidos' spiritual movement against gang violence.*
        *by* AARON GALLEGOS

To Break the Chains of Violence ......................................49
*Building community and self-esteem.*   *by* BREAK AND BUILD

Safe For Youth.....................................................................50
*What your church can do.*     *by* YVONNE DELK

**STAFF**
...................................................

*Executive Director,* Jim Wallis
*Publisher,* Joe Roos
*Editors,* Aaron Gallegos, Kelly M. Green
*Managing Editor,* Karen Lattea
*Art Director,* Ed Spivey Jr.
*Associate Editors,* Bob Hulteen, Kari J. Verhulst
*Assistant Editors,* Rachel Johnson, Jeremy Lloyd
*Development Team,* Hugh E. Brown III, Nancy Maeder,
        Elizabeth Holler Hunter
*Director of Marketing,* David A. Wade

*Cover photo by Jim West*

# STREET BLESSING

## When violence comes home.

*by Jim Wallis*

Well, it finally happened. After more than two decades of living and working in many of America's meanest streets, I was mugged. As a veteran urban pastor, organizer, and even a gang truce adviser, I'm embarrassed to say that they took me by surprise. It was only 6 o'clock in the evening—during rush hour. I suppose I watch my back better after midnight. But these guys were so fast and bold, I'm not sure it would have made any difference.

Needing a few things at the store before an early morning flight, I headed out to my pickup truck parked at 13th and Fairmont Streets NW, right around the corner from where I live in D.C.'s 14th Street corridor.

Looking over my shoulder in response to the sound of running feet, I saw four young men bearing down on me. The first one hit my slightly turned head with something sharp enough to open a cut above my left eye. The force of the blow and a push from two others sent me to the pavement. One of them yelled, "Keep him down! Get his wallet!" It finally registered. These guys were trying to roll me over.

I popped up quickly, which seemed to surprise them. Seeing no weapons flashed, I squared to face my attackers. This was the first chance we had to really see each other face to face. They were just kids—three about 15 or 16, and one little one who couldn't have been more than 13.

The boys backed up a little when they saw I was bigger than they had expected. I'm a strong believer in nonviolence, but have learned that being a weightlifter often helps in these potential confrontations. The one who had hit me moved into a boxing stance while the others circled. The little guy began attempting some ineffectual karate kicks, which I assumed he had seen on television.

Intending not to hurt them, only to fend them off, I instinctively began to scold these lost young souls. I told them just to stop it, to stop terrorizing people, to stop such violent behavior in our neighborhood. Finally I shouted at them, "I'm a pastor!" And I told them if they wanted to try to beat up and rob a pastor, they should come ahead.

Maybe it was my desire to confront these kids with what they were doing and give a personal identity to their potential victim. But invoking the authority of the church in the street is hardly a sure thing these days, when our churches often have such little involvement in those streets.

Whatever it was that changed their minds, my assailants turned and ran. "Get back here," I shouted after them—then instantly realized it probably wasn't a good thing to say at that point. But then something unusual happened.

The littlest kid, who couldn't have been more than 4 foot 6 inches tall, turned back to look at me as he ran. With a sad face and voice, the young karate kicker said, "Pastor, ask God for a blessing for me."

He and his friends had just assaulted me. The little kid had tried so hard to be one of the big tough guys. Yet he knew he needed a blessing. The young boy knew he was in trouble.

Here were young people demonstrating social pathologies that make them a very real threat. Yet they are themselves also vulnerable and alone. Their dangerousness should not be underestimated, as some socially concerned individuals who live at a safe distance sometimes do. On the other hand, these young perpetrators are much more than just social pathologies, as some politicians in Washington, D.C., seem to imply.

Driving to the doctor to get stitched up, I was especially conscious of other people out walking, many just coming home from work, and most more vulnerable than I am on the street. So many potential victims of my gang of four. All these people deserve to be safe on the streets of their own neighborhoods and city. That must be a bottom line to which we commit ourselves.

But we must also commit ourselves to those kids. They too must become our bottom line. What they need most is nurture, discipline, and a real opportunity. Many of them have none of those right now. And as long as they don't, our streets will get more dangerous.

How do we rebuild the relationships, structures, and environments that provide these essentials for our young people? The current Washington rhetoric of "cutting them off and locking them up" won't do it. And it's certain that what's needed is beyond just what the government can do. This will take all of us—our families, churches, and communities. It will test our moral resolve and political will and require both the private and public sector to become involved in new and creative ways. No one gets to opt out.

The violent behavior of street criminals must be stopped. But the four young men who attacked me are more than just criminals. They are also children—our children—and they are in a great deal of trouble. The violence will only be turned around when the young people who now roam wild are included in our future. Young people who feel like they are part of society's future will not be attacking the rest of us on the streets. If we can find the ways to include them, we will all receive a blessing. ∎

*JIM WALLIS is editor of* Sojourners *magazine in Washington, D.C.*

**Questions:**

■ *What would be your response if you or a loved one were victimized in an incident of street violence? Why?*

■ *Do you agree that anonymity contributes to violence in our society? What are some ways we can "personalize" our city streets?*

■ *Often we demonize those we don't know, especially if we are frightened. Do you find yourself making assumptions about people you see on the streets? Is there a way to be "street smart" without having a cynical edge?*

# RESISTING DEATH INCARNATE

## The principalities of urban violence.

*by Bill Wylie-Kellermann*

*Slowly I learned something which folk indigenous to the ghetto know: namely, that the power and purpose of death are incarnated in institutions and structures, procedures and regimes—Consolidated Edison or the Department of Welfare, the Mafia or the police, the Housing Authority or the social work bureaucracy, the hospital system or the banks, liberal philanthropy or corporate real estate speculation. In the wisdom of the people of the East Harlem neighborhood, such principalities are identified as demonic powers....* —**William Stringfellow**, *Instead of Death* (1967 ed.)

By his own account above, late street lawyer and theologian William Stringfellow was first alerted to the reality of the principalities by his friends and clients in East Harlem, who experienced an array of predatory social forces invading and occupying their neighborhood. His subsequent years of lucid biblical reflection on "the powers" began in a certain sense with his friends' intuitive theological street wisdom.

Where churches begin to engage the violence now invading and occupying our own urban neighborhoods, a theological analysis of the principalities and powers may prove crucial. On the one hand, it enables a biblical way of naming and thereby seeing what is sometimes called the "structural violence" targeted with uncanny vitality against the urban poor. And on the other, it explains, like nothing else, the street-level violence (now mushrooming out of control) that people turn upon one another. And beyond both, it may suggest certain spiritual resources the church must claim in this struggle—which truly "is not against flesh and blood, but against principalities, against powers, against the rulers of the darkness of the world, against spiritual wickedness in high places" (Ephesians 6:12).

In a theological nutshell, Stringfellow came to recognize these institutional powers as "creatures" having an independent life and integrity of their own. Each—the banks, the police, the welfare

> **Humans who wield violence and imagine they control it are actually in bondage to it. They have become its minions and servants and victims.**

bureaucracy—stands before the judgment having a concrete vocation to praise God (as with all creation) and to "serve human life" in a particular way. However, in the idolatrous inversion of the Fall, these incorporate creatures instead imagine they are God and enslave human life. Idolatry and the Fall means the servants have become masters and overlords of domination, thus becoming predatory, dehumanizing, violent: They incarnate the power and purport of death.

TO TAKE ONE of Stringfellow's examples, the police, who sometimes advertise on the side panel of their cars (virtually as an echo of their true vocation) that they purport "to serve and protect," may function in the Fall as an occupying army. In the Fall they protect not people but economic boundaries, serving not human life but property.

Or, to take another, the welfare apparatus, whose very name suggests a vocation of wholeness, health, well-being, even justice ministered to individuals and families, ends up operating for the management and control of the poor. Procedures, by sluggish indifference, humiliate and dehumanize. The system discourages self-reliance and entraps people in a cycle of poverty. Bureaucratic regulations implement family breakdown. Assistance amounts are all but designed to finance misery on the brink of survival. Boundaries of social geography are enforced as people are relegated to a narrow range of overpriced, run-down housing in which they will never hold equity. All of this is violence, what may be called the power of death incarnated.

Or consider the banks, local offices of a commercial principality participating in the global economy. In Detroit, there is a bank that ran an ad campaign some years back averring itself to be the bank "where the bottom line is you." This, of course, is a bold-faced deception: At that financial institution, it is the bottom line which is the bottom line. Once again, in the ad some vague notion, a haunting commercial memory, remains of what the vocation of a bank ought to be.

A bank that serves human community would, for example, make people's consolidated resources available to the neighborhood as credit. Instead, the banks sometimes struggle even to comply with the barest legal requirement that they reinvest credit

locally. Instead, they enforce social boundaries by redlining whole neighborhoods. Instead, they function to "steal" the community's collective resource, investing it by a complex scheme in some other part of the world entirely. Invariably, human beings on both ends of the scheme are being disempowered and enslaved.

These days, one must mention the weapons-makers as an urban power. This domestic weapons complex, largely based in New England, boasts a $16 billion annual market. Its chain of marketing and distribution principalities—legal and illegal—includes some 287,000 licensed gun dealers in the United States, and of course one of the most powerful political lobbies in Washington, D.C., the National Rifle Association, to keep the product flowing. There are currently 200 million firearms loosed on the streets of our country.

STRINGFELLOW, SPEAKING of his experience 30 years ago, alludes to the Mafia. One thinks of a scene from *The Godfather*: The Dons sit at table debating the wisdom and morality of a mafioso entrance into the drug business. It is a dispute already threatening war among the families. The Marlon Brando character steps forward with authority to deliver the acceptable compromise: We will sell heroin, but only to Negroes. Needless to say, the drug system has come a long way since. It has developed into a notorious principality of urban violence.

To comprehend drugs as a power means, at a minimum, to see it whole, as an entity, a configuration of competing underground corporations, economic arrangements, illegitimate operations, and cultural forms. It means seeing the complex system of transnational-national enterprises.

As an economic entity the system reaches across the planet. Between the poppy or coca fields and the hustling street vendor lies this huge enterprise. In certain respects it is a network marketing

**D**onald Trump paid $89,000 to take out ads saying, "I hate these kids. I want everyone to hate these kids....BRING BACK THE DEATH PENALTY!" (in response to the Central Park Jogger "wilding" incident).
—*Encyclopedia on Violence*

operation (of the variety mastered legally by Amway) with a 700 to 2,000 percent mark-up from one end to the other. Moreover, it conforms to the patterns of the two-tiered global economy. Above, elites dominate production, manufacture, and global export, with a middle-management operation overseeing regional distribution, para-military security, money laundering, and the like. Below are the peasant farms (Third World raw materials) and the crackhouses or their equivalent feeding on cheap labor. Once again, on either end, people are held in bondage. Notice too that on both ends the same weapons, the same methods of enforcement, the same violence proliferates.

Legally it's an elaborate conspiracy, but as with any structural power, the whole is greater than the sum of its parts. Like Adam Smith's invisible hand, it takes on a life of its own, claiming those who claim to control it. Moreover, since it operates illegally (the free market truly unleashed), it has a phenomenal vitality, an inordinate versatility.

For example, at street level the crackhouses on my block a few years back could rapidly shift their mode of operation from infrastructure support (with runners for the open drug bazaar in the park) to drive-up operations going night and day. The social traffic pattern and even the personnel can change, but it is the same operation. Jailing a "kingpin" changes nothing: It's not a conspiracy, but a structural power.

Gangs, especially the so-called "corporate gangs," regularly engage the global economy through the drug system. A gang, at a certain scale, may itself be considered in its aspect as a principality, a collective entity with a life of its own. Like nations or banks or bureaucracies, gangs too stand before the judgment of God.

Vocationally, they are turf-based powers taking responsibility for a certain neighborhood or housing project. They are, I suppose, called to praise God and serve human life through that territorial responsibility. Instead, of course, in the fallenness of

human life, gangs regularly end up invading and occupying (not to mention defacing) the very neighborhoods they are called to serve; they enslave young people into their membership; they serve the corporate interests of the drug system; they mark human beings for violence. It is like nothing so much as redemption, for which we may give thanks, that certain gangs now reclaim their calling.

THERE IS, HOWEVER, an urban power that must also be named in this list of examples: violence itself. It may be of a different order. It is not so easy to think of it as a creature with a vocation, but it does, beyond question, have a life of its own, and certainly a spirit.

Violence is a human capability which—in the alienation of human beings from God, from one another, and from themselves—becomes a power unto itself, closely akin, if not synonymous, to the power of death itself. As with other principalities, humans who wield violence and imagine they control it are actually in bondage to it. They have become its minions and servants and victims.

Jacques Ellul, the French theologian and social historian, has articulated certain of the mechanisms by which this takes place. He is considering particularly military, political, and revolutionary violence, but his insights will have street recognition. Ellul urges a realism about the necessary laws by which violence always operates:

1) The law of continuity: Once you start using violence, you cannot get away from it. It simplifies relations by denying alternatives. It is the way of the street; there is no way out of it.

2) The law of reciprocity: You enter into a reciprocal relationship capable of being renewed indefinitely—the famous cycle of violence. Structural injustice breeds street violence which breeds police brutality which breeds....

3) The law of sameness: Condoning one kind of violence endorses and condones all others. This is why violence "escalates" practically without limit. The brush becomes the fight becomes the gang-bang becomes the turf war. The fist becomes the knife becomes the handgun becomes the Uzi.

4) The law of justification: Those who employ it always justify it. I was a victim. It's survival. It

> **"W**olves, after all, were like people. If you feared them, and ostracized them, they eventually turned into what you were afraid they were anyway."
> —Murray Bodo, *Francis: The Journey and the Dream*

was righteous.

5) Violence begets violence, and nothing else. (To claim otherwise is blindness and the big lie.)

Realistically, says Ellul, these are laws. And not only the law of the street. They are the mechanisms by which violence as a power takes on a life and momentum and direction of its own—how it stalks the street and the planet. These laws hold and bind: They are the bonds of our slavery to violence. They are the logic and order of necessity. (For Ellul, "necessity" is virtually a philosophical synonym for the Fall and its bondage).

Where this is understood, the gifts of faith are summoned into play. What is required in the main is freedom—freedom to break the laws of violence, freedom from the kingdom of necessity. That freedom is a gift of God alone, and is the very thing the life of the church, the life of a Christian, bears witness to. It will be expressed theologically in a variety of ways, but comes down to the same reality. It may be called the forgiveness that breaks the cycle of violence, or the grace that alone justifies, or the love that overcomes. It may be called the miracle that the powers would convince us is impossible, or the hope of things not seen that subverts the rule of despair. Above all it will be called the resurrection of Christ, which is freedom from the power of death.

Any plan or program not rooted in that freedom will succumb to the laws of violence, the order of necessity, the way things are.

Stringfellow glimpsed the freedom of the resurrection years ago in East Harlem.

*Resurrection is verified where rebellion against the demonic thrives....I am not being romantic in using Harlem as symbol, particularly when I refer to Harlem in rebellion signifying the resurrection. I am, however, affirming that in the black ghetto there is a resistance to death as social purpose, a perseverance in living as human beings, a transcendence of the demonic which is at least an image of resurrection which exposes and challenges the reign of death in this society and which, thus, benefits all human beings.* ■

*BILL WYLIE-KELLERMANN, a* Sojourners *contributing editor, is a United Methodist pastor teaching at the Whitaker School of Theology in Detroit. His most recent book is* A Keeper of the Word: Selected Writings of William Stringfellow *(Eerdmans, 1994). This article adapts portions of his "Shadow, Mirror, and Mime: Drugs As a Power," from the May 1992 issue of* Sojourners.

**Questions:**

■ *Do you believe the heart of the problem of violence is a spiritual issue? What does that mean to you?*

■ *How does our society perpetuate violence? Are we truly a people enraptured by violence? If not, why are we studying and addressing it? What is wrong with violence? Is it part of human nature?*

# 'TAKE YOUR INHERITANCE'

## The challenge before the churches.

*by Eugene F. Rivers III*

More than 10 million black people now face a crisis of catastrophic proportions. Life in American inner cities is poor, brutish, and short; and future prospects are even bleaker.

Unlike many of our ancestors, who came out of slavery and entered this century with strong backs, discipline, a thirst for literacy, deep religious faith, and hope born of that faith, we have produced a generation that does not "know the ways of the Lord," a "new jack" generation ill-equipped to secure gainful employment even as productive slaves. This generation provides unique insight into current economic opportunities.

Consider this achievement: A generation of poor black men, women, and children may reach the end of this century in a position worse than their ancestors who entered the century in the shadow of slavery. Unable to see a more rational future through the eyes of faith, they lack the hope that sustained their forebears. Lacking hope, they experience what sociologist Orlando Patterson has called "social death." But unlike the social death of slavery, this new social death is fundamentally spiritual. Rooted in the destruction of faith and hope, it produces a world in which history and identity are themselves divested of meaning, a world of nihilism and despair.

What, in these unprecedented circumstances, are the responsibilities of the churches—and black churches in particular? One observation is especially pertinent.

The pathologies of the cities are essentially an advanced expression of a more general crisis of moral and cultural authority that currently overshadows the lives of all black Americans born between 1950 and 1970. The black churches are not exempt from this crisis. Our blind pursuit of the false gods of the American Dream has come at the expense of institutional and political autonomy.

Lacking such autonomy, we are entangled in a web of inherited ideological and political assumptions—for example, an incoherent conception of rights divorced from moral obligations. Living on borrowed assumptions, we face moral and cultural obsolescence. In a tragically proverbial sense, we are now a church bereft of a vision.

Yet, for the people of God, every crisis, no matter how grim, presents a unique opportunity that can only be seen with the eyes of faith. For example, in racially war-torn Boston, black, Roman Catholic, and Jewish clergy have come together by faith to develop concrete strategies for reducing the material basis for crime and violence among the black poor. Black clergy who are members of the Ten Point Coalition hit the streets by faith, going into crack houses and gang-infested areas at night to reclaim our children (see "A Call to Action," page 43). By faith, academic institutions such as the Center for Values and Public Life at Harvard Divinity School and the Andover Group of Andover Newton Theological School are devising practical methods for integrating theology and social policy to produce outcomes-oriented programs at the grassroots level. At this unprecedented time in the history of black people, God is bringing forward new wineskins into which the new wine of vision, power, and hope is being poured.

If the black church is to be faithful as the church of Christ, larger numbers of clergy and laity need to join the ranks of those being filled with the new wine of God's power. To be the force of spiritual renewal and transformation that the black church has historically been, we must put Jesus first and heed his call:

*Come, you who are blessed by my Father; take your inheritance, the kingdom prepared for you since the creation of the world. For I was hungry and you gave me something to eat, I was thirsty and you gave me something to drink,...I was sick and you looked after me, I was in prison and you came to visit me (Matthew 25:34-35).*

Let us live exemplary lives devoted to Christ and to serving our brothers and sisters. On the streets are young people who are struggling to live upright lives in a corrupt age, as well as those whose rebellion against the victimization of our community led them into illicit activities. As clergy we can encourage our congregations to join us in working with our youth.

Let us as clergy and laity together embrace the youth, disciplining our young people and confronting them with the gospel and the love of Jesus Christ, remembering that whatever you do for the least of these brothers and sisters, you do for Jesus (Matthew 25:40). ■

*EUGENE F. RIVERS III, of Azusa Christian Community in Boston, is a fellow at the Center for Values and Public Life at Harvard Divinity School and a member of the coordinating committee of the Ten Point Coalition.*

## Questions:

■ *Eugene Rivers cites Matthew 25:34-35 as a call for the church to serve urban youth. Who are those in your life that need this sort of attention? Do other passages of scripture come to mind when you confront the problem of violence in our society?*

# BEHOLD THE NONVIOLENT ONE

## A peacemaking journey through the beatitudes.

*by Mary Lou Kownacki, O.S.B.*

*If you have inner peace, thousands of people around you will be saved.*
                                        —St. Seraphim

St. Seraphim makes it sound so simple, yet it takes a lifetime of concentration to become a true peacemaker, a peacemaker like the one described in the following story:

*When the Chinese invaded Tibet, many of the soldiers were especially harsh and mean-spirited toward the monks. Upon their arrival in one village, the Chinese invaders heard that all of the monks had fled to the mountains except one.*

*The commander raged out of control. He marched to the monastery, kicked in the gate, and sure enough, in the courtyard stood the one remaining monk. The commander approached the monk and screamed, "Do you know who I am? I am he who can run you through with a sword without batting an eyelash."*

*The monk gently, but steadily, gazed at the commander and replied, "And do you know who I am? I am he who can let you run me through with a sword without batting an eyelash."*

The monk is my model of a peacemaker. Behold the nonviolent one: disarmed, centered, vulnerable, detached, unafraid of death.

The question the monk poses for us is this: How do we become people of peace? How do we become a church of nonviolence? What experiences in life, what methods of prayer prepare us to stand disarmed? Jesus, I think, shows us a way to become a people of peace.

In the Sermon on the Mount, he offered the beatitudes as steps toward a disarmed heart. The beatitudes, in other words, might be seen as a series of stages that Christians must pass through if their spirituality is to mature and deepen to the point of total disarmament.

### BLESSED ARE THE POOR IN SPIRIT

THIS FIRST BEATITUDE is the beginning of the spiritual journey. To be poor in spirit means that you can say in truth, "I am a worm and nothing." To be poor in spirit means that you can say in truth, "I am God." Or as the rabbis in the Hassidic movement teach, we should all have two pockets. In one is the message, "I am dust and ashes." In the other is, "For

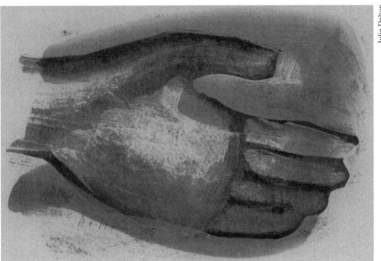

Julie Delton

me the universe was made."

The spiritual journey begins with awakening to what it means to be human or it never begins at all. To become aware of creaturehood is to grasp this tale: I walked up to an old monk and asked him, "What is the audacity of humility?" The old man answered, "The audacity of humility is to be the first to say, `I love you.'"

God is audaciously humble. God is the first to say, "I love you."

Awakening to gratuitous love is ground zero in the spiritual life. Oh, wonder of wonders! God first loved me. God made a unilateral initiative. I did not merit this gift: to be made by love and in love. In a sense, the miracle of being a beloved child of God is an insight from which the mystics never fully recover. "Just to be is blessing, just to live is holy," exclaims Rabbi Heschel. To be poor in spirit, then, is to know my dignity as a child of God and to recognize the same God in my brothers and sisters.

> "**W**hen others are weeping blood, what right have I to weep tears?"
> —José Martí,
> 19th-century Cuban writer

### BLESSED ARE THEY WHO MOURN

THIS GROWING AWARENESS of the sacredness of all life plunges the follower of Christ into the second beatitude, "Blessed are they who mourn."

It is one thing to wax poetic about the sacredness of life, another to plant your feet on earth in the 1990s. It is no exaggeration to image the world as a gaping wound. The church pictures it in more poetic

"**N**onviolence is the answer to the crucial political and moral questions of our time; the need for humankind to overcome oppression and violence without resorting to oppression and violence."
—Martin Luther King Jr.

terms: a vale of tears.

Some of the sorrow is beyond our control, but the more we analyze the stories behind the newspaper headlines, the harder it is to hide from harsh reality. Our apathy, our lifestyles, our budget priorities mean mourning and weeping for tens of millions around the globe.

But to mourn the disfigured face of God is not enough. We must also learn to walk through this bitter valley and make it a valley of springs. Somehow we must immerse ourselves in the turmoil and tears, enter deeply into the pain, and yet walk lightly through it, leaving a wellspring behind.

The poor in spirit—those who recognize the sacredness of life and they who mourn—those who realize the violence under which so many live—face a dilemma: How do we restore dignity, how do we bring wholeness to those denied basic human rights? How do we bring forth that day "when every tear shall be wiped away and death shall be no more, neither shall there be crying nor pain anymore?"

### BLESSED ARE THE GENTLE

SOME, OF COURSE, advocate violence to right the wrongs. But the beatitudes suggest an alternative, another way to engage in the struggle. And that alternative is the third beatitude, "Blessed are the gentle."

Another translation for this beatitude is "Blessed are those who do not use force." The next step in the spiritual journey, then, is the invitation to nonviolence.

The spiritual power of nonviolence is what Mohandas K. Gandhi called "soul force," while the Christian speaks of a "power of love" that can overcome the world. To accept the invitation to nonviolence is to begin living out of a disarmed heart. The beatitudes that follow this one suggest or explain what is involved in the nonviolent way of life.

### BLESSED ARE THOSE WHO HUNGER AND THIRST FOR JUSTICE

THE FOURTH BEATITUDE, the one immediately after the invitation to nonviolence, is, "Blessed are they who hunger and thirst for justice."

This beatitude reminds us that nonviolent love is always other-centered and public; nonviolence takes place in the streets as well as in the cell of one's own heart. To begin the journey of nonviolence is to find oneself hungering and thirsting after justice and being drawn actively to resist any system or government that diminishes life.

This is where the Catholic bishops of the Philippines found themselves in the '80s after the fraudulent Marcos elections. They called an entire nation to resistance, endorsing a protest campaign that included prayer and fasting, boycotts, vigils, strikes, demonstrations, and civil disobedience.

Who will ever forget "People Power" and hundreds of thousands on their knees, facing guns and tanks, armed only with rosary beads, Mary statues, and flowers?

If ever you need to explain the fourth beatitude, bring the Filipino people to mind. To hunger and thirst for justice is to take concrete action. It is an active refusal to submit to injustice and an active showing of love.

### BLESSED ARE THE MERCIFUL

IT IS ONE THING to resist the structures of violence and quite another to serve the victims of institutional violence. That is why the next beatitude, "Blessed are the merciful," moves the spiritual journey to another level.

Nonviolent love includes unconditional love, a willingness to serve others without counting the cost. It involves a total pouring out of self, a day-by-day dying to our own agendas, dreams, and priorities.

About 20 years ago, I was part of a group that opened a center for nonviolence. At first we thought nonviolence meant sponsoring seminars and workshops on the topic and organizing nonviolent actions against the war system.

But it wasn't until we started a soup kitchen and began welcoming the homeless into our lives that we began to understand the implications of the nonviolent cross. I would be less than honest if I didn't admit that direct service to the poor is the one element of nonviolence that I struggle with constantly. That said, I must insist that the most important thing I've learned over the past 15 years is this: Some direct contact with the poor is indispensable for those who call themselves peacemakers.

First, it is imperative to have some kind of presence next to the "least" of God's children if we are going to speak to others about peace and justice with any credibility. More important than giving us public credibility and a sense of personal integrity, though, is what the poor will teach us about ourselves and, consequently, about God.

It is in rubbing shoulders with the poor, the marginal, the lonely, that our nonviolence is tested as gold in fire. The words of Jean Vanier warn of a danger all too prevalent among peace and justice professionals: "Is not one of our problems today that we have separated ourselves from the poor and the wounded and the suffering? We have too much time to discuss and theorize and have lost the yearning for God which comes when we are faced with the sufferings of people."

### BLESSED ARE THE PURE OF HEART

THE NEXT BEATITUDE, "Blessed are the pure of heart," comes as a surprise. Here we thought action—signing petitions, marching in the streets, writing letters to government officials, and even committing civil disobedience—would make us peacemakers. We thought serving soup to the hungry and preparing beds for the homeless would bring in the reign of God. Instead, we discover that all the killing and destruction, all the pain and screams, only reflect our inner violence, our own lack of inner peace.

What a startling insight: Conversion of heart must accompany conversion of the world. The problem is purity of heart. Now we must wrestle with the demons within. The words of Thomas Merton haunt us: "Instead of loving what you think is peace, love other men and women, and love God above all else. Instead of hating all the people you think are warmakers, hate the appetites and disorders in your own soul which are the causes of war."

It is through daily conversion, through fasting and solitude, that we grow in truth. We become radically honest with ourselves and others, meeting face to face all the lies and fears, hatred and harm that spring from self-righteousness and pride.

Gradually, we grow in understanding of the person we truly are in God's sight. The film that covers the eye of our heart completely dissolves and we can see each man and woman as they are in the eyes of God. The beauty of that reality is blinding. Everywhere we look, we behold the face of God.

## BLESSED ARE THE PEACEMAKERS
FROM THIS contemplative vision flows the next beatitude, "Blessed are the peacemakers." They are called children of God, those who recognize the unity of the human family. One who is pure of heart, one who sees the face of God in every human being cannot injure, cannot kill, cannot comprehend the term "enemy." One who sees the whole world in a single ray of light cannot speak of nation states or superior races or inferior sexes. The peacemaker has a single vocation: to keep the vision of oneness, of wholeness, of God's unconditional love for all alive in the marketplace.

Wherever there is injustice, discrimination, division, or violence, we should find peacemakers, God's children. Where the battle rages between the forces of light and darkness, we should find peacemakers, God's children. And God's children enter the public arena, the conflict, trying to make God's love visible.

This means that we love our enemies as ourselves, we accept suffering without retaliation, we meet hatred with love. "Rivers of blood may have to flow before we gain our freedom," Gandhi told his followers, "but it must be our blood."

## BLESSED ARE THE PERSECUTED
THIS FINAL THOUGHT brings us back to the foot of the cross and to the final beatitude, the final stage of the spiritual journey: "Blessed are those persecuted for justice's sake."

> "**W**e are constantly being astonished at the amazing discoveries in the field of violence. But I maintain that far more undreamt of and seemingly impossible discoveries will be made in the field of nonviolence."
> —Mahatma Gandhi

Suffering love first attracted me to nonviolence. I can remember watching the evening news in the early '60s, staring transfixed at the African Americans who sat at segregated lunch counters and refused to move until they were served, while angry whites poured ketchup on their heads, smeared mustard through their hair and eyes, and pelted them with racial slurs.

I heard the word "nonviolence" and wondered how people could absorb such hatred without striking back. Then I read an account in *The Catholic Worker* newspaper where an African-American man was quoted as saying: "I will let them kick me and kick me until they have kicked all the hatred out of themselves and into my own body, where I will transform it into love."

That unidentified black man let me see the cross of Jesus anew. No longer was it possible to see the death of Jesus as a mere historical event, a dogma of faith to adhere to but never connect to real life. No, the disarmed figure on the cross was an invitation to me to break the cycle of violence, to be an instrument of continuing redemption through suffering love.

A seeker, it is said, searched for years to know the secret of achievement and meaning in human life. One night in a dream a Holy One appeared, bearing the answer to the secret. The sage said simply, "Stretch out your hand and reach what you can."

"No, it can't be that," said the seeker. "It must be something harder, something more satisfying to the human spirit." The sage replied softly, "You are right, it is something harder. It is this: Stretch out your hand and reach what you cannot."

Can we reach for something harder, something more satisfying to the human spirit? Are we ready to risk the gospel? Can we chance all we are on the beatitudes? Can we follow the nonviolent Jesus? Dare we—all of us together—stretch out our hands and reach what we cannot? ∎

*MARY LOU KOWNACKI, O.S.B., is a* Sojourners *contributing editor and a Benedictine sister living in Erie, Pennsylvania.*

## BIBLE STUDY:
Matthew 5:1-12, Luke 6:20-28.

**FURTHER READINGS: Way of Peace: A Guide to Nonviolence**. Edited by Gerard Vanderhaar and Mary Lou Kownacki. Pax Christi USA, 348 East 10th St., Erie, PA 16503.

## Questions:
■ *Does living a disarmed life mean offering one's own presence as a deterrent to a violent situation? In your opinion, does this mean we must actively restrict the ability of others to act violently?*

■ *The Tibetan monk brings to mind a popular phrase within the nonviolence movement: There are many things worth dying for but none worth killing for. Is it inherently against human nature to be willing to die without batting an eyelash? Do you believe the "soul force" of nonviolence has the power to disarm others?*

■ *Read the beatitudes. What do they mean for you? Do you believe all Christians are called to follow them today? Why or why not?*

# WORTH FIGHTING FOR

## *The churches mobilize to save urban America.*

*by Jim Wallis*

**Boston.** A young man fleeing two pursuers with automatic weapons ducks into a church during a worship service, believing he will be safe there. His assailants don't even pause at the church door as they rush in and open fire. The choir stops singing, the preacher dives under the pulpit, and the congregation crouches beneath the pews as the sanctuary is sprayed with bullets.

Later, at a press conference, church leaders indignantly decry the blasphemous violation of holy thresholds and sacred space. But Azusa Christian Community's Eugene Rivers, an African-American street pastor, offered a different and prophetic word: "If the church won't go into the streets, the streets will come into the church."

**Washington, D.C.** All the Sunday morning talk shows focus on out-of-control violence in the United States. Nobody is safe, says a worried-looking David Brinkley. Desperate politicians and police chiefs talk crime bills and gun registrations and the president speaks of the breakdown of work, family, and community. What's most clear is that the political and media elites haven't got a clue as to what to do. Sunday night, the children living in the capital of the world's last remaining superpower go to bed to the sound of gunfire.

**Palestine, eighth-century B.C.E.** The prophet Isaiah delivers oracles to the children of Israel and to the neighboring Egyptians about the plight of their societies:

*Their land is filled with silver and gold, and there is no end to their treasures; their land is filled with horses, and there is no end to their chariots. Their land is filled with idols; they bow down to the work of their hands, to what their fingers have made. And so the people are humbled; and everyone is brought low.*

The consequence, the prophet continues, of a society's greed, social injustice, and idol worship is judgment in the form of

> **In some neighborhoods a black male between 15 and 24 is more likely to die by gunfire than was a U.S. soldier in Vietnam.**
> —Margaret D. Canio, Ph.D.

spiritual degradation, violence, and the break-up of community. The people turn on one another, "they will fight, one against the other, neighbor against neighbor, city against city, kingdom against kingdom." The people's "spirit" will be "emptied out" (Isaiah 2 and 19).

I WILL NEVER FORGET a conversation with some young Crips and Bloods in Watts after the Los Angeles riots in 1992. When asked what the churches could do to help, an 18-year-old gang member looked us straight in the eyes and said: "We need the churches to lead us to the Lord." I now believe that in responding to this call the churches themselves will be led back to the Lord.

> **T**he escalation of violence on our nation's streets has reached such a crisis that perhaps only the religious community can adequately respond to it.

The escalation of violence on our nation's streets has reached such a crisis that perhaps only the religious community can adequately respond to it. Why? Because the cruel and endemic economic injustice, soul-killing materialism, life-destroying drug traffic, pervasive racism, unprecedented breakdown of family life and structure, and almost total collapse of moral values that have created this culture of violence are, at heart, spiritual issues.

The frightening disregard for human life among too many young people is a bitter reflection of the way these same young people have become so utterly disregarded by their society. The coldness of heart that now makes even veteran urban activists shiver is a judgment upon our coldness toward our poorest children. We reap what we have sown.

Neither liberal sociology nor conservative piety can begin to address the roots of this crisis. Neither government spending nor simplistic self-help slogans will suffice. What is called for now is that particular biblical combination of which the prophets most often spoke—*justice* and *righteousness*. Both the structures of oppression and the morality of personal behavior must undergo radical transformation. We need a change of heart and a change of direction not only among troubled urban youth, but for all of us.

BECAUSE SPIRITUAL transformation will be at the absolute core of the changes we so urgently need, the churches must help lead the way. But such a leadership role will first require some soul-searching on the part of the churches. This problem is too deep and our task too large to take it on by ourselves.

Dan Hubig

anti-violence initiatives of several denominations, national organizations, and local churches. The vision that came out of this gathering is very practical. Local churches and congregations must connect with youth organizations to create positive and concrete steps toward conflict resolution and community development. Local churches need to be encouraged to apply the ancient idea of sanctuary in creating open and safe spaces in the midst of urban war zones.

Primary attention needs to be focused on the necessity of community-based economic development as an alternative to lethal drug trafficking and as a way to solidify inner-city neighborhoods. Ecclesiastical structures should be challenged to make money and investment portfolios available for that crucial task. Church portfolios are currently worth $35 billion, but only a fraction of 1 percent of that is invested in community-based development.

Local churches are called upon to become actively involved as advocates for young people in the criminal justice system. Churches should be enlisted in the very controversial task of keeping both drugs and guns out of their communities. Pastoral resources must be specifically applied to the epidemic of sexual irresponsibility and abuse, as well as to the central task of family reconstruction.

We will need the help that comes "by faith." As another young man in that post-riot meeting in Watts said to us, "We've got some habits that only God can cure." That goes for all of us.

The contribution of faith communities to a social crisis always comes precisely at the point of perceived lost causes and hopeless circumstances. The writer of the Letter to the Hebrews says that "faith is the substance of things hoped for, the evidence of things not seen" (11:1). Or, as I like to paraphrase it, hope is believing in spite of the evidence, then watching the evidence change. At critical historical junctures, faith makes possible the political imagination to find solutions to seemingly impossible social problems.

Hopeful signs are already apparent.

At the Kansas City, Missouri "Gang Summit" in April 1993, participants came back again and again to the need for "spiritual power." All seemed to agree that political and economic programs, by themselves, were inadequate to the depth and enormity of the urban crisis. In addition, virtually all the "observers" and "advisers" invited to the summit by the 164 current and former gang leaders were from the religious community (see "A Time To Heal, A Time To Build," page 26).

In November 1993, those companions to the Kansas City summit met again to strengthen church-based support for the gang truce movement and the

Any strategy that does not highlight the centrality of evangelism and spiritual transformation is doomed to failure. The evangelical agenda of the gospel must be made dramatically clear in the power of God to transform people's lives. Resources also need to be made available to help local churches biblically interpret the "signs of the times" in our present crisis and to find the most faithful and practical ways to respond.

AT SUCH a critical moment, churches must also take the risk to become vitally involved in advocacy on behalf of policy issues that affect children,

Why "war zone"? Emergency room doctors in our cities are now using techniques developed during the Vietnam War to heal wounds from assault rifles. The MLK-Charles Drew Medical Center in Los Angeles offered its emergency room to the Army for training surgeons in battlefield conditions.
—*Encyclopedia of Violence*

for example. At the same time, they must eschew the partisan and ego clashes that inevitably attend such a political crisis. Churches must take the moral high road that leads to grassroots action.

Groups around the country are connecting for the sharing of organizing models. In Kansas City, the "Break and Build" program grew out of the Gang Summit and is turning young gang members toward peace and jobs. The Evangelical Lutheran Church of America is offering critical resources and technical assistance for new projects initiated by Barrios Unidos in Santa Cruz, California (see "'We're in the Forgiving Business,'" page 44).

A powerful network of mostly black evangelical urban ministries, the Christian Community Development Association, is offering new hope for both evangelism and economic development in cities across the country, and the Catholic bishops' Campaign for Human Development is making possible myriad community organizing projects. At the Sojourners Neighborhood Center in Washington, D.C., at-risk inner-city children learn not only educational and conflict resolution skills, but also how to be "freedom fighters" in the tradition of their African-American forefathers and foremothers. A coalition of urban churches in Boston is offering a 10-point plan for citywide church mobilization that provides one concrete example of what could be done around the country (see "A Call to Action," page 43).

The key to all these efforts is the willingness to move our faith into the streets. Neither big steeple churches nor storefront congregations can afford to wait on young people to come in their doors. We must go to them.

Recently, members of a prominent black Baptist church in Washington, D.C., spoke to me of how

**W**hat is called for now is that particular biblical combination of which the prophets most often spoke—justice and righteousness.

they sorely wanted to reach out to their neighborhood, but didn't know how.

"Almost none of us live here anymore. Maybe some of us should move back," offered one church elder. "The kids on the streets don't have the clothes to come to our church. They don't feel comfortable given the way we all dress," another woman said.

In response, the church decided on a December "come as you are" Sunday, when everyone would be encouraged to wear ordinary clothes and the youth who hang out on the streets outside would be invited in. "If it works, we might all have to change," noted a church member.

In the face of escalating urban violence, we begin with the work of prayer and the fervent conviction that our children are worth fighting for. As hopeless as things may seem and as helpless as we may feel, we must claim the sight that comes by faith in believing that our kids are not a lost cause, that violence will not have the last word, and that as the Bible asserts, "death will have no dominion."

"This is our time," says Jean Sindab, a longtime church activist. Who else can better step into the breach that has grown up in our society? States Sindab, "It is a time for the church." ■

*JIM WALLIS is editor of* Sojourners *magazine in Washington, D.C.*

## ORGANIZATIONS:

**Operation Break and Build**, 2000 E. 12th St., 2nd floor, Kansas City, MO 64127; (816) 842-7080.
**Christian Community Development Association**, 3827 West Ogden, Chicago, IL 60623; (312) 762-0994.
**Sojourners Neighborhood Center**, 1323 Girard St. NW, Washington, DC 20009; (202) 387-7000.
**Campaign for Human Development, U.S. Catholic Conference**, 3211 4th St. NE, Washington, DC 20017-1194; (202) 541-3210.

# SANCTUARY IS MORE THAN ARCHITECTURE

*The church as safe place.*

*by Yvonne Delk*

In order for our young people to secure the right to have options other than drugs, gangs, and guns, they must find safe space—for love, employment, and protection. The church is called to act now with a sense of moral urgency to provide this sense of safe space.

### THE REALITY
WE CONTINUE TO LOSE a whole generation of our young people in a violent culture and context. Here is a look at their reality:

■ Children and youth of our nation are dying on our streets, in roller-skating rinks, in schools, in homes, and on playgrounds.

■ Many of our children cannot play in playgrounds or sit on their front porches without fear of a bullet piercing their skulls.

■ The escalation of violence on our nation's streets has reached epidemic proportions. Young black men ages 15 to 24 are six times more likely to be killed than other Americans of similar age.

■ Almost all of our communities are facing a crack cocaine crisis of epidemic proportions. Every seven minutes a child is arrested for a drug offense.

■ Twenty-five percent of young black males between 23 and 29 are in prison. More black males are incarcerated at some stage of the criminal justice system than are enrolled in institutions of higher education.

■ Every 53 minutes a child dies because of poverty.

■ Every eight seconds an American child drops out of school.

■ Many of our young people face daily the lures of drugs, sex, fast money, and guns; these are the unnoticed youth who operate in a maddening universe where things always seem to go wrong.

■ Our children and our youth are not being educated, nurtured, matured, or disciplined in their hearts, minds, and bodies.

John Spragens Jr.

"**T**he churches must learn humility as well as teach it."
—George Bernard Shaw, 20th century Irish dramatist and critic

## THE CALL

THE CHURCH IS CALLED to be safe space. In this space young people and children are no longer named by the culture of violence or nihilism, existing with no meaning, no hope, and no love. Rather, the church becomes the free space where they find identity and value, a faith to preserve, the courage to resist oppression, and love that can lift, motivate, and inspire them to claim and contribute their skills, abilities, and talents.

In the sanctuary of this environment, they are surrounded and connected to mentors and a community where they can be rooted in their history and gain strength, direction, and purpose for their lives and for the building of safe and just communities.

## THE BLACK CHURCH

THE BLACK CHURCH IN America has been safe space for African Americans. It is the one autonomous, independent, and free institution within the black social order representing a vitalizing beacon of hope and opportunity. The black church has served as an anchor for African-American families since the horror of the transport from Africa to the Western Hemisphere.

For those living in a society where racism was (and continues to be) an assault on their dignity and worth as persons, the black church was the space that affirmed them as persons and offered them the freedom to be and build community. The black church offered the free space to grow, develop, and reach for and accomplish dreams. It was a center of hope and affirmation, containing the power to speak world-changing words that created a new self-respect and the ability to act with dignity, self-determination, and interdependence. It became the overwhelming "yes!" in the nihilistic sea of systemic and personal oppression.

## A PERSONAL TESTIMONY

I GREW UP IN MACEDONIA African Christian Church in Norfolk, Virginia. It's my model of free space. For it was there that resistance to white injustice was joined with faith in God's righteousness. When my father, who dug graves at Calvary Cemetery Monday to Friday, entered the door of Macedonia he was more than a gravedigger, he was Deacon Delk. When my mother, who worked as a maid, entered our church on Sunday morning she was Sister Delk.

It was in this safe space that my parents, my sis-

"*The brothers don't attend church all the time, but they know the door is open. They come in with their hats on and their pants sagging because I've given them an invitation: You come through that door when you're ready.*"

**—Jerry McAfee, Baptist preacher, United for Peace in Minneapolis**

ters and brothers, and I were freed from the nihilistic experience of a hostile environment where all the forces of culture combined to say to us that we were nobody or nothing. It was there that the preached word and the lived word of the extended family intersected with our identity crisis and struggle. It was there in Sunday school, in the young people's choir, in the youth fellowship meetings, surrounded by the support system of mentors and spiritual guides, that we were able to transcend the circumstantial realities, the cultural realities, and even the law of the land.

We were empowered to name ourselves from the perspective of faith, meaning, hope, and love. We were no longer orphans or objects; we were the daughters and sons of God, created in God's image.

Macedonia was free space. It was the source of our identity and survival. It sustained us as a family. We were the people of God whose future was not defined by the negative structures that humiliate us. In this sacred space, the value structures in society were completely reversed in the free space of the church. The last became first, the gravedigger became the chair of the deacon board and the maid became the president of the deaconess board, and I and my three sisters and three brothers received the strength and courage to pursue our dreams. ∎

*YVONNE DELK is executive director of the Community Renewal Society (332 South Michigan, Chicago, IL 60604; (312) 427-4830).*

## Questions:

■ *Name some times that you have felt others were treating you as God's son or daughter. Name some times when you have been treated as less than God's child. What lessons can we learn from our own experience for how we treat the "stranger" in our midst?*

■ *The church has long been a "safe space" for ethnic groups in the United States. What cultural changes have threatened the church's ability to provide this service? What theological changes in the country have undercut this calling?*

■ *How is your church a "safe space" for its members? Is it a "safe space" for you? How can you extend that safety to others? What are some of the things you can do to make your church more welcoming?*

# IN JESUS' NAME

*Azusa Christian Community reclaims the poor and dispossessed in Boston.*

*by Anthony A. Parker*

It was so sad, yet so unsurprising. Several members of the Azusa Christian Community in Boston had gathered on the corner of School and Washington Streets to pray for Robert Smith, better known as "Man," who was shot a few nights before on that same corner. While we were gathering to pray, a fight broke out up the street. Two women were determined to break a bottle over the head of a man and maybe the woman he was with, too. Several of our group ran over to intervene. The police were called. They arrived after the fighters had already left.

No one in the group knew why those women and the man were fighting, cursing, screaming, and willing to tear off their clothes in the freezing weather and snow. That kind of rage and anger—the kind that disappears as quickly as it erupts—is dangerous. It requires a healing that secular institutions and good works alone cannot offer.

So our little group prayed. We prayed for "Man," for the spiritual salvation of the people fighting, and for the collective soul of our black community.

The Azusa Christian Community is an intentional community of black men, women, and children who are committed to the complete renewal—spiritually, culturally, intellectually, and politically—of the black poor people in inner-city Boston. The members of Azusa—most of whom were educated at Harvard University, the Massachusetts Institute of Technology (MIT), and other elite academic institutions—choose to live among the black poor in the Four Corners and Codman Square neighborhoods in North Dorchester. While holding down full-time jobs to support themselves and their families, or while struggling through graduate school, the members of Azusa still find time to act as surrogate parents for an ever-expanding army of angry, emotionally unstable young black people.

Given the deteriorating circumstances of the black poor and the alienation between urban black youth and older mainstream black leadership—especially within the black church—it is a particularly thorny proposition to inspire young black people to seek justice in Jesus and in the Bible. But such is the task and calling of Azusa.

Named after Los Angeles' Azusa Street, where the first black Pentecostal church was located in the early 1900s and where the first pentecostal explo-

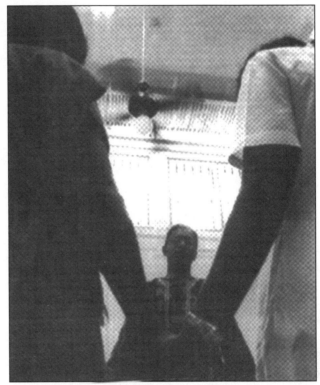

*Eugene Rivers, center, leads a prayer at Azusa Christian Community's Sunday worship service.*

Photos by Terry O. Gross

sion in the United States was sparked during a revival preached by William J. Seymour in 1905, Azusa takes its call seriously. It is a daily challenge that may find some of its members in court, in public schools, and in the streets, bearing witness to the fact that "our struggle is not against flesh and blood, but against the rulers, against the authorities, against the powers of this dark world and against the spiritual forces of evil in the heavenly realms" (Ephesians 6:12).

AZUSA'S CALLING IS to bridge three worlds: the biblical, the political-economic, and the cultural. The Dorchester Uhuru Project is the formal name given to Azusa's street ministry. Based on aspects found in the Christian-led Southern Freedom Movement and the Student Nonviolent Coordinating Committee's Mississippi Freedom Summer project, the Uhuru Project is a multifaceted

> "What we say is coming from what we know—not what we hear, or what we think, but what we see. I saw someone dead on some steps of a school I used to go to....I didn't hear that, I saw that."
> —Yocca Risen,
> high school student, Kansas City

**"W**hile there is a lower class, I am in it; while there is a criminal element, I am of it; while there is a soul in prison, I am not free."
—Eugene Debs, labor organizer

*At right, Eugene Rivers talks with probation officers outside Dorchester Municipal Court.*

campaign designed to organize citizens around those issues most critical to their everyday lives—health care, public safety and crime, education, employment, and adequate housing.

Azusa seeks to empower black youth by first attempting to instill discipline and Christian values in them. "Our vision over the next five years is to evangelize 1,000 young blacks," states Azusa pastor and founder Eugene Rivers. "We are working to develop a new movement—new organizational models and forms of evangelism that are explicitly Afrocentric."

The point person for outreach on the streets, Eugene states bluntly, "Virtually all churches fail to impact the urban black male ages 18 to 35. That's who we are specifically targeting for evangelizing."

Azusa's concentration on outreach to poor black men is based on the fact that it is they who are murdered in highest numbers, incarcerated in highest numbers, have the lowest life expectancy of any group in the country. "It was the poor black mothers, sisters, and daughters of black men that encouraged us to go organize among the black males," Rivers said.

Perhaps, but pain does not discriminate, especially in the inner city. "There's a lot of woundedness around the issue of gender on all sides in the black community," according to Jacqueline Rivers, an elder in Azusa. Jacqueline is director of the Boston office of the Algebra Project, a national organization that focuses on making algebra easier for inner-city middle school students to understand. "For a lot of black women, it's an experience that doesn't permit you to be what is your concept of a woman, because you must be man and woman at the same time."

Twenty-one-year-old Sophilia Robinson lives in Mattapan. She has a 2-year-old son, Marquis, and reflects the tension between being black and female in the inner city. "I've seen you all [Azusa] working with the boys because they need the most help. They're the ones out on the corner, selling and shooting and doing all that.

"But the girls need just as much help," Sophilia continued. "Teen-age girls need to know not to have children now; they need to know to go to school. For those single mothers who do have kids, there should be some kind of workshops. You can get stressed out by having so many responsibilities. Some sort of program to help them find jobs, to get them off welfare, to make them want to finish school and do something for themselves."

Michelle Shaw, a Harvard-trained lawyer, left a high-paying job downtown to work in a small law firm located across the street from Dorchester Municipal Court in Four Corners. She has spent considerable time, energy, and expense at "being there" for several 15-year-old girls from nearby Jamaica Plain—Sherell Johnson, Kendra Johnson, and Latara Green. For instance, Michelle attended the girls' graduations from middle school this summer—in some instances, standing in for a parent or other relative who could not come. With the breakdown of the traditional family, increasing violence in the schools, drugs, rising numbers of teen-age AIDS cases among blacks, and a blatantly sexually permissive culture, it is imperative that Christians step in to help parent this generation of black children.

Another aspect of Azusa's work is the Community Youth Technical Exchange Program (CYTE). A summer program in its third year, CYTE is run by Alan Shaw, a Ph.D. candidate in computer science and media technology at MIT and head of his own company, Imani Information Systems. CYTE teaches neighborhood youth how to fix basic electrical appliances and offer their services to the residents of Four Corners for a small fee. Also taught through CYTE is computer use, electronic trouble-shooting, and graphic design.

The youths make a set of business cards for themselves, set goals for themselves, and work on following through on their commitments to the neighborhood. Individual initiative and achieve-

ment, neighborhood economic clout, a skill, and confidence in one's ability are just a few of the values learned through CYTE—values necessary for the survival of any at-risk community in the country. Many of the computers are donated by various groups, and the city of Boston has given CYTE funds to help keep the project going.

THE DORCHESTER municipal court, the busiest in the city, is located in Four Corners. Every weekday morning, from the time it opens until its doors close, the courthouse bustles with young black and Puerto Rican men waiting for their turn to appear before the judge.

"Too many of our young people are in prison. As Christians we can't give up on them," says Eva Thorne, a graduate student in political science at MIT. Eva is involved with Azusa's Youth Advocacy Project, which tracks at-risk youth in close consultation with probation officers, lawyers, and judges. "For the gospel to be truly life-transforming and powerful, it should be able to reach the most despised among us," says Eva.

The growing number of young black men who have dropped out and remain unemployed provides ample evidence of the education system's failure. And many of the teen-age women one sees walking along the streets have small children in tow—their fathers in jail, in the hospital, on the run, or dead.

Can you imagine death without the assurance that being a Christian brings? Death comes at an early age for too many black young people today. And Four Corners is no different.

This thought occurred to me as I sat outside the chapel of a funeral home in Mattapan on a cold rainy evening. I was at a wake, with several other community members, for a man I had never met. Only 36, he had died of AIDS. I knew his two nephews, "Y-Dawg" and "B-Boy." Both have shared space on my living room floor. It is a poignant and scary realization that even the most hardened black youth can be tamed by death's shadow; something always expected but never quite prepared for.

LIVING IN THE INNER CITY is a pain sometimes. Like when my family's car and Michelle and Alan's car were hit by half a dozen bullets during a drive-by shooting. But we at Azusa are integration's success stories. Most of us have undergraduate degrees, have or are completing master's or doctoral degrees. Our income or income potential is excellent. We are, if you will, the "house Negroes," sharing space on the same plantation with the "field Negroes."

The culture of Harvard and MIT fosters an exclusivity that is not easily broken. Being black is

# Fueled By The Spirit

**THE HALLMARK** of Azusa's ministry in Four Corners is the belief that salvation is the greatest equalizer. "Azusa's organizing and evangelism is the object of an intensified corporate prayer life. Understanding the role of the Holy Spirit is one of the most vital dimensions of our ability to minister successfully at the corporate and individual levels," notes Rev. Eugene Rivers.

"The level of violence in these inner cities requires a level of spiritual power so intense that we encourage folk who don't understand the importance of the Holy Spirit for ministry not even to bother. All that could possibly happen is that you will get worn out or run out," says Eugene.

He should know. Two years ago, more than a dozen bullets crashed through the windows of Eugene and Jacqueline Rivers' home, one of them missing their son's head by an inch as Malcolm slept in his bed.

To effect meaningful change, Azusa recognizes the need to take spiritual authority over the demonic forces ruling Four Corners. Emphasis on conversion and spiritual growth reflects Azusa's quest to move beyond political analyses and community service.

In 1984, when most of the members of the then-African People's Pentecostal Church were still undergraduates, the three main pillars of their worldview were food distribution, political campaigns, and intellectual discourse. Although Christians, their spiritual maturation had not yet caught up with their political and intellectual acumen.

The Azusa Christian Community has evolved from a Harvard Christian student organization known as the William J. Seymour Society to a maturing church of about 20 adults and a score of children and teen-agers. Azusa is an eclectic bunch: Single mothers, a police officer, a lawyer, the owner of a computer software company, and educators. Most live within a six-block area in Four Corners and Codman Square, with some living in Roxbury and Cambridge.

All Azusa meetings are definitely charismatic. Singing, praying, and general sharing are loud and enthusiastic and not for the faint of heart. Regular attendance at services and community meetings are vital to Azusa's ability to function as "a voice of one calling...prepare the way of the Lord" in Boston.                                    —AAP

> "**P**eople say, what is the sense of our small effort? They cannot see that we must lay one brick at a time, take one step at a time."
> —Dorothy Day, author and co-founder of the Catholic Worker

*At right, an Azusa women's group meets for reflection and prayer.*

not necessarily an advantage in trying to evangelize among the poor and disadvantaged—when you are neither, and when you may sound different, look different, and have no concrete or intuitive feel for the rhythms of hardcore black life, or street life in general. As Azusa begins to expand and perhaps take on a working-class flavor, a clash of two cultures is imminent.

How Azusa prepares for this future is critical as new leadership is groomed to handle its urban ministry. Ultimately, the true test of discipleship, as lived in the context of community, is the challenge to young, gifted, and educated black men and women—like the people in Azusa—to communicate with their less educated, less stable black peers.

"Approach means everything to people who live different from the people in Azusa," says Anna Young, a community member since 1990 and an invoice clerk at Boston's Children's Hospital. "The people we are trying to reach will turn everyone else off on us if we don't approach them correctly." Young sees her role in the community as being a credible bridge between the worlds of Harvard and MIT and the people whose world is defined by the streets. "[Azusa] cannot be seen as poverty pimps," says Young.

"I think one of the most significant components of the education I received here, in the fellowship, has been around the issue of class," Jacqueline Rivers said. "I think we can become one with the poor. But I think we have a long way to go. We have to rely heavily on the Spirit of God and God's ability to love through us, guide us, and to correct us in everything we do. God's ability to transform is the key. We've had a lot of time to work that out, just among ourselves. We've had personality issues just among ourselves that obviously have a bearing on how we'll relate to people outside."

There is a consensus in the community that the estrangement between black elites and the black poor can best be resolved through relationships. Eva Clarke, a former elder in the church, says, "As a woman, I have a different focus in dealing with class issues than the men. I think with women there's some common ground that we can capitalize on—especially regarding children.

"Women want something better for their chil-

dren. So that's a bond. After three years of living in this neighborhood, it seems that I'm able to begin to know people better and to establish some relationships. I anticipate some success in dealing with people just in respecting them, communicating concern and love for the women in the neighborhood."

Azusa's commitment to the biblical mandate to serve the poor is coupled with the other biblical command to conversion—an acknowledgment that any change in a person's circumstances must begin with God. The act of conversion is empowering in ways that simply feeding the hungry, clothing the naked, and housing the homeless are not. Freedom must start at the individual level, with a personal experience of transformation, and then move upward to the family, through the church, and finally spill over into the wider community. Azusa understands this much: The purpose of community is Christ-centeredness. ∎

*ANTHONY A. PARKER, a former* Sojourners *assistant editor, is a teacher living in Dorchester, Massachusetts. He is a member of Azusa Christian Community.*

## "We have all known the long loneliness, and we have learned that the only solution is love and that love comes with community."

### —Dorothy Day

**FURTHER READING:**

**Beyond Rhetoric.** National Commission on Children, 1111 18th St. NW, Suite 810, Washington, DC 20036.

**Fire From Heaven: The Rise of Pentecostal Spirituality and the Reshaping of Religion in the Twenty-first Century.** By Harvey Cox. Addison-Wesley Publishing Co., 1995.

**The Liberating Spirit: Toward an Hispanic American Pentecostal Social Ethic.** By Eldin Villafañe. William B. Eerdmans Publishing Co., 1993.

**Questions:**

■ Parker says the estrangement between the rich and the poor can best be resolved through relationships. What implications does this have for the way we approach our youth at risk?

■ The Azusa Christian Community believes that salvation comes as an individual experience first, which is why they stress a conversion-based Christianity. Is that true in your experience? How do your beliefs around the conversion experience compare? Share a conversion experience you have had.

■ What does sound political analysis and a commitment to social service do to help change the lives of those who are most at risk in urban America? How might those at risk contribute to the effort to devise policy to curb violence in our society?

# BEING CHURCH IN THE 'HOOD

## Developing "Young Men With A Future."

*by Elizabeth Perpener*

It was "battlefield time" again for Raymond Blanks. The Director of Public Policy and Social Advocacy at the Ohio Council of Churches had just arrived at Shiloh Baptist Church in Columbus, Ohio, to meet with the first participants in the Young Men With A Future program.

The young men came from the near east side of the city, from private homes and public housing projects, from single and foster parents, and from traditional families. They included Methodists, Catholics, Pentecostals, and Baptists, but almost half of them belonged to no church at all. Ranging from 13 to 17 years old, some of the young men wore fashionable fade haircuts while others preferred being bald. They interacted loudly during a supper of homemade lasagna, fruit salad, chocolate cake, and Gatorade.

Once supper was over, the boys rapped a chant of appreciation to the women of Mt. Vernon A.M.E. Church who had prepared the meal. The youth then went to the church's auditorium where Dr. Michael Williams, a professor of psychology at Dayton's Wright State University, would engage them in a learning session focused on strategies of violence prevention.

At Young Men With A Future, nothing begins before prayer is offered. The devotion and prayer segment signaled the start of the serious business the teen-age boys would be engaged in for the next two hours. "Young men will have no future unless they are anchored and awed by God's presence in their lives," Blanks commented.

During intercessory prayer one youth shyly prayed for his grandmother and another followed. One boy petitioned in memory of young men murdered in a drive-by shooting. Finally, one youngster lifted up those everywhere who abuse any kind of substance or are in prison. The cadre of elders also offered their petitions, especially for the teen-agers

> " I hope you'll hear this call. We need you. We have to change that suffering, change that negative into positive and use that to move forward. We need to nourish our men in the reality of things, and show them that we need them back in the family, not gangbanging, selling drugs, or imprisoned. We need them at home, with us, side-by-side."
>
> —MaryLou Rangel, Barrios Unidos

involved in the ministry to young, at-risk African-American males. Everyone responded to each petition, "Lord, have mercy."

Dr. Williams began by bellowing mockingly to the youth, "What's up?" He then proceeded to describe the increasing dominance of violence in the nation's inner cities, cogently mixing hip street lingo with classroom English. Too many young men have been taught they must be tough and in control, he said. The results of such macho behavior, he emphasized, have been deadly. Violence is not caused by drugs or alcohol or poverty only, Williams said, but violence is about power, a power that lusts for control yet results in increasing division, danger, and death among black youth.

After capturing their interest, Williams drove home his primary point: Violence can be prevented by the choices young people make. He urged, "Self-control is the most basic responsibility and the most basic form of all power." Everyone, he cautioned, can exercise real power and choose to control themselves.

The young men interrupted to question Williams' assumptions and presented him with examples of typical challenges they confront frequently in their neighborhoods. Williams then walked up to a youth and got in his face to demonstrate how to avoid arguments or fights. He urged the youth, with pleading tones of seriousness, "Don't let anybody make you mad, make you argue, or make you fight." Before he departed, the boys rose with beaming faces and applauded Williams for his challenging presentation.

RAYMOND BLANKS STARTED Young Men With A Future after reading a distressing 1990 report from the Ohio Commission on Socially Disadvantaged Black Males on the social plight of his brothers in the Buckeye State. Black men are too frequently unemployed. They represent the greatest

Jim Hubbard

"Are the investments in our children expensive? Compared to what?"

—William S. Woodside, corporate CEO

**"** **I**f you love those who love you, what reward will you get? Are not even the tax collectors doing that? And if you greet only your brothers, what are you doing more than others? Do not even the Gentiles do that?"

**—Matthew 5:46-47**

numbers of those murdered or in prison and they rank at the lowest level of life expectancy. Too many, the state report documented, have dropped out of school and society before becoming adults. For Blanks, the crisis impacting black men presented an opportunity for the church to be directly involved in reducing and reversing their diminished status.

At Blanks' urging a task force was organized by the Ohio Council of Churches in 1991 to elevate black men from their status of crisis. The council realized that its commitment to disadvantaged African Americans added integrity to their ministry of redemption and liberation. Rev. Harvard Stephens Jr., pastor of St. Philip Lutheran Church in Columbus and a former chaplain to incarcerated teens in Baltimore, became the chair of the council's task force.

Blanks urged Stephens to tap into his experience and to author a Christian values curriculum specifically designed to be relevant to young black men. Months later, and after many hours of meetings, revisions, and valuable criticism from a consulting education specialist and a psychologist, the 60-page curriculum was completed. Since its publication, more than 2,500 copies have been sold to churches in Ohio and across the nation seeking to enhance their moral education programs in the African-American religious community.

The curriculum, according to Stephens, is "designed to bring young African-American teenagers into conversation with the word of God and to expand their ethical horizons." Stephens and Blanks felt a more powerful witness by the religious community was required to make a positive difference. "It was past time for us as the church to take our faith into the streets of Columbus and to serve our youth by walking the walk rather than only talking the talk," Blanks remarked.

Schools failed too many. Families found themselves in the greater difficulty of nurturing and protecting their children.

The idea of community had eroded and social systems and institutions proved more inefficient as their resources also decreased amid increasing demands. The church too needed to confront the social challenge facing youth at risk.

Blanks and Stephens saw that the problems of black youth were not only social but also spiritual. Black teens desperately needed right values in their struggles for survival in more difficult times. They decided that a direct program of intervention by the church community that focused on the personal development of black youth was urgently required in dangerous times of drugs and drive-by shootings.

YOUNG MEN With A Future is a 10-week, Afrocentric social skills development and spiritual formation program sponsored by 10 churches of various denominations and other local religious groups. "By specifically targeting young, black men as the focus of evangelism," Blanks explained, "we're trying to become a more visible and viable force of faith—the church in the 'hood."

Blanks and Stephens got 10 other ministers to join in the initiative. The pastors agreed to revise their annual budgets to contribute to the program's costs. This cooperative approach made it easier for each church to become involved without their resources being over-taxed.

An innovative program like Young Men With A Future adds a critical dimension and further

Jim Hubbard

STUDY SESSION 2

expands the church's service to all the people of God. Many inner-city youths emerge from broken families and wounded communities that too often fail to provide the essential human and spiritual experiences that foster healthy growth. A great danger facing many people among the underclass of the inner-city is their social isolation from mainstream society and the corresponding degrees of hopelessness in the midst of overwhelming problems. Stephens and Blanks feel that ministries such as Young Men With A Future could contribute to healing the social divisions now more apparent in the African-American community. Since 1993, a similar program involving seven congregations serves 50 youths in Dayton, Ohio.

The youth service program signals to the community the churches' determination to be a source of refuge and strength during a time of despair and decline. Special programming to young men by this coalition of churches demonstrates the capacity of the community of faith to close the gap between those who have and those who do not.

Both participants and parents have been encouraged by the new sign of life represented by this program of faith and works inspired by love. The youth in this program know that people beyond their families care about them as people who matter, and that their community has high expectations of them. They now know their community will help raise them.

Says 14-year-old John Lane of the program, "I needed to know some facts about becoming a man." He said it was helpful "to have quality time and learn about ourselves, our culture, our people, and our pride. The program helped me understand another way of learning."

SINGLE MOTHERS ALSO benefit from this type of programming focused on strengthening young men spiritually. The youth become involved with mentors who are not only solid role models but who also demonstrate an example of social responsibility for the common good. Mentors watch over their charges, encourage persistence in their pursuits, and coach them to be as wise as serpents and as gentle as doves. The mentors are, Blanks explained, living icons of black men who struggled against great odds to survive and succeed.

"With the breakdown of the concept of community and the escalation of chaos in our cities, it is even more imperative that the church step in and

*Our approach to the dilemma of youth violence is unique; it is based upon the belief that community workers who have experienced and overcome the challenges facing young people today are best able to assist them in choosing life-affirming behavior. This kind of behavior is based on positive self-esteem and cultural pride. Developing a collaborative, non-traditional approach is a must if we are to solve these problems.*
—Daniel "Nane" Alejandrez and Otilio Quintero, Barrios Unidos

stand with families as they battle against the powers of this world and spiritual forces of evil, including pernicious public policies and adverse social practices," Blanks insisted. He added, "The church can at least be a safety zone offering viable alternatives to danger, despair, violence."

Most important for Stephens and Blanks is that they have taken a leap of faith and acted on their conviction that the gospel is never only personal but also has profound social implications. "The good news," Blanks added, "is that God is also working with us and changing us as we seek to be his servants among the forgotten." The Christian faith, he maintains, "must struggle to be where it belongs, on the side of the weak, the disinherited, and among victims of injustice, and even with the boys in the 'hood."

The final day of the program was spent at an amusement park in northern Ohio. As the caravan of church vans returned to Columbus, George Powell, the staff member also known as the "Fun Captain," shouted out:

*They say black men
will sell you drugs or shoot ya.
But not us,
cause we're young men with a future!*

It is now more likely that the 40 participants will indeed become black men with a future because the church served and cared for them, showed them a more excellent way, and taught them essential spiritual and social lessons for their struggles and survival. ∎

*ELIZABETH PERPENER is a free-lance writer focusing on religion and social issues. She lives in Westerville, Ohio. The National Council of Churches in Christ selected Young Men With A Future as the recipient of the 1993 Ecumenical Recognition Award, which recognizes projects that address the systemic issues that cause brokenness. Recently, the Ohio Council of Churches received a grant to replicate Young Men With A Future in Cincinnati, Cleveland, and Youngstown.*

**RESOURCES:**

**Young Men With A Future,** an Afrocentric, Christian values curriculum designed for young African-American males, is available for $5 per copy (plus $1.50 for postage) from the Ohio Council of Churches, 89 East Wilson Bridge Road, Columbus, OH 43085; (614) 885-9590.

**Questions:**

■ Have you tried to approach young people in your community? Working with youth can be very frustrating. What are signs of success for you? What are your expectations of results? What is enough for you to deem a project "worth it"?

■ Young Men With A Future focuses primarily on young men. What is the significance of this kind of program for women? What are parallel ways to reach out to young women?

■ Have you ever benefited personally or professionally from working with a mentor? Have you ever been changed as a result of being a mentor to someone else? What do people need to share their experience, gifts, and skills with others?

A FAITHFUL RESPONSE TO URBAN VIOLENCE                    25

# A TIME TO HEAL, A TIME TO BUILD

## *Lessons from the Gang Summit.*

*by Jim Wallis*

*Sojourners' editor Jim Wallis was one of a number of people invited to participate as an adviser at the National Urban Peace and Justice Summit, which took place April 29 to May 2, 1993, in Kansas City. This "Gang Summit," as the event has come to be known, was the first in a series of such gatherings held around the country.* —**The Editors**

It was an "altar call" unlike any you've ever seen. Two young men from rival street gangs—one a Crip and one a Blood—came together at the pulpit in St. Stephen's Baptist Church. The two confessed they had been trying to kill each other for more than a year. And then the enemy gang members "dropped their colors" at the pulpit and embraced each other, tears in their eyes.

From now on, they said, they would walk the same road together. Enough killing—it was time for a new beginning. For a gang member to drop a kerchief or piece of clothing with their gang's colors is a momentous thing. One can be killed for such an act. But it was not the only momentous thing that occurred in Kansas City that weekend.

*Participants at the Gang Summit pledge their commitment to end violence.*

Jeff Scott

From a "truce" that began between the Crips and the Bloods in Los Angeles several months before that city's 1992 spring rebellion, a "truce movement" had begun to spread in other cities across the country. Before long, connections were made between the various "gang peace" efforts and a kindred spirit began to grow.     The initiative for the gang truce movement and the summit came from the young people themselves in the ghettos and barrios. Expressing disappointment in the established political, civil rights, and church leadership, they decided to act on their own. The date chosen was the one-year anniversary of the first verdict in the Rodney King case and the subsequent uprising in Los Angeles.

One hundred and sixty-four current and former gang leaders and members from 26 cities, and 53 observers, gathered in Kansas City for an event that could be viewed as a historic turning point in the life of America's cities. Most of the nation's largest and most powerful urban gangs were represented— Crips, Bloods, Vice Lords, Black Disciples, Gangster Disciples, Black Souls, El Rukhns, Cobras, Stones, and Latin Kings.

While other national leaders call for an end to the violence on our streets, this was a gathering of people who potentially have the power to stop it. These young men and women represent the possibility of a new generation of leadership from the war-torn streets of the nation's inner cities. The National Urban Peace and Justice Summit brought a new sense of unity and responsibility among them.

## NOT SEPARATE, BUT TOGETHER

GATHERED together were tough gang leaders and former felons, young men who had already served years in penitentiaries, those who had lost many family members and friends, people who had themselves committed terrible violence against others. These very intense days were fraught with tension, ego, controversy, and conflict. What held the Gang Summit together and ultimately overcame many obstacles was a common passion to end the killing.

"Our barrios are suffering. We come here for peace. We're tired of seeing our mothers come to the graveyard," said Daniel "Nane" Alejandrez of Santa Cruz, California, the executive director of the National Coalition of Barrios Unidos, to the assembled crowd. Summed up one teen-age gang member: "We would rather live than die; it's as simple as that."

"We are on a mission," proclaimed Fred Williams, a youth worker from Watts who has been a pivotal figure in the Los Angeles gang truce. "It's time to get down to business."

While summit participants came from many cities, they also came from the same place of deep pain. Mac Charles Jones, one of two host pastors, offered the welcome and invocation at St. Stephen's Baptist Church: "We are here to make our pain mean something. We want our pain to be redemptive."

A sort of gang leaders "banquet" the first night had the feel of a family reunion. People introduced themselves to each other—Crips meeting Vice Lords, Latin Kings meeting Bloods. People who had been fighting on the streets and killing each other for years were now talking, finding shared experiences, making new friendships, and developing joint strategies.

Perhaps of greatest significance was the coming together of African-American and Latino gangs and agendas. "Black and Brown!" became a constant chant. "Racism has driven us apart," cried one speaker. Participants in large numbers came from both African-American and Latino communities, and the real commitment to diversity was evident in speakers, issues, language, and cultural expression.

A sense of unity grew, born of similar experience at the hands of a "white system" and of common problems to resolve. Fred Williams and Nane Alejandrez, as the summit's co-chairs, exemplified the new and exciting possibilities. The Gang Summit was dedicated to the memory of César Chávez, who drew respect from brown and black alike.

T-shirts created by United for Peace in Minneapolis announced a much repeated slogan: "Apart We Can't Do It, But Together We Can." Unity did not come easily in Kansas City, and it was evident to most participants that it will not be won on the streets back home without a great deal of work. Yet unity was stressed as the key to progress. "Let's Fly to a Better Place" proclaimed a rainbow-emblazoned banner. A new peace sign was adopted by Gang Summit participants. Instead of a "V" sign with fingers held apart, the same two fingers are uplifted and held together—"not separate, but together."

AN UNEXPECTED TURN on the question of unity came with the emergent role of women at the Gang Summit. At an earlier planning meeting, the handful of women present made a strong contribution, prompting Vice Lord Minister of Justice Sharif Willis to say, "Brothers, we have heard things from our sisters that we didn't understand before. They've told us things we didn't know, and they've made us better understand who we are and where our real power comes from. Brothers, we need to bring more sisters to this summit."

....................................

*"It was powerful to know the strength of women, and that our strength is relevant."*

—Najma Nazy'at, community organizer in Boston

Jeff Scott

# THE SISTERS' STATEMENT

WE ARE THE MOTHERS, THE SISTERS, THE GIRLFRIENDS, AND THE GANG BANGERS. WE HAVE TO GROW TOGETHER.

WE MUST BE EQUAL PARTICIPANTS. WE MUST BE ABLE TO SPEAK UP WITHOUT BEING CONDEMNED OR SILENCED. OUR AGENDA IS THE SAME AS YOURS.

AS WOMEN WE HAVE ALWAYS KNOWN VIOLENCE. IT IS GANG BANGING AND POLICE BRUTALITY, BUT IT IS ALSO DOMESTIC VIOLENCE, RAPE, CHILD ABUSE, AND POVERTY.

WE INSIST THAT WOMEN ARE APPROPRIATELY REPRESENTED ON ANY ADVISORY GROUP OR BOARD OF DIRECTORS DEVELOPED OUT OF THIS SUMMIT. WE ARE OUR BEST RESOURCES. NO AMOUNT OF MONEY IN THE WORLD CAN ACCOMPLISH WHAT THE STRENGTH, INTELLIGENCE, AND LOVE IN THIS ROOM CAN. WE HAVE TO POOL OUR SKILLS.

THE MOST IMPORTANT ISSUE IS THAT WE WORK TOGETHER. WE LOVE YOU AND SUPPORT YOU. OUR EFFORT IS ONE. ■

Fifty "sisters" were there, but they were all but ignored the first day by the "brothers" and by the media who only wanted to interview male gang leaders. But then the women stepped forward. Marion Stamps, a longtime community organizer from Chicago's notorious Cabrini-Greens projects, had challenged the Daley machine and city power structures for many years; she was not about to be intimidated now by male gang leaders. After the tragic shooting of a young boy in her housing project, she had become a midwife of the Chicago gang truce.

Established leaders joined with the younger sisters in a closed women's caucus. They emerged with a statement for their brothers and took an active role in the rest of the summit (see "The Sisters' Statement," above). As one young woman described it, "Our place is not behind you, or under you, but beside our brothers in this struggle."

## STRATEGIES TO REBUILD

POLITICAL SELF-CONSCIOUSNESS was prevalent at this gathering. "Gang-related violence isn't the only violence," said many participants. One young man described his experience: "I have to go to school without books. That's violence. I watch TV programs which degrade my people. That's violence. I never see anyone in power who looks like me. That's violence."

Some put the issue bluntly, saying this summit was not just about ending gang-related violence so white people in the suburbs could feel safer. It was about stopping the senseless killing, so people could get on with rebuilding their own communities.

A full day's program was devoted to planning a strategy of community-based economic development, dealing with police brutality, creating new visions and values to strengthen families and neighborhoods, and empowering and raising up new leadership.

The economic development goals went far deeper than just hustling jobs on the fringes of the corporate economy. Creating alternatives to the lucrative and lethal drug traffic, the mainstay of gang economic activity, was a high priority.

Most people were talking about the development of small projects, businesses, and cooperatives that would serve the community and be accountable to it. The idea of community-owned and -operated enterprises created much more enthusiasm than obtaining franchises from corporate giants.

Bobby Lavender, a convener of the economic development task force and from South Central Los Angeles, said, "We have to lift the community out of poverty, not just individuals. We have to be motivated by more than just making money and then the money will follow." Lavender, who is now suffering from cancer, added, "If you don't look out for the whole, and just look out for yourself, you're eventually going to lose out."

The relationship between gang members and the police departments of their cities is an arena of great conflict and mistrust. The sessions on police brutality were filled with stories of harassment, surveillance, intimidation, terror, physical and sexual assault, the use of attack dogs, torture, and even executions at the hands of local police.

Recommendations for protecting inner-city youth and improving their relationship with the police included the creation of communi-

ty-based citizen patrols to monitor police activities. Of special concern was the status of 15,000 police brutality cases that have languished for many months and years and the spate of new anti-gang legislation, said to deprive its targets of their civil rights.

"IF YOU DON'T LOVE yourself, you can't love anybody else," said several young people. Self-respect, self-esteem, and self-control were ideas so frequently mentioned it sometimes felt like a self-help convention. In many ways it was.

There was as much strong talk during the weekend about improving the quality of human relationships as there was about economic development, as much concern for personal transformation and individual character as for political change. The weekend continually defied traditional categories.

No word was more often heard than respect. "Don't disrespect your brother or sister" was a continual refrain. Respect is what these young men and women have felt the least of from their society; it is what they most seek for themselves and their communities.

The closing summit statement spoke of personal as well as social responsibility in finding empowerment. By understanding and claiming their cultural heritage, these men and women feel they can restore traditional values and ways of doing things, strengthen families through effective parenting, and take responsibility to create healthy and safe environments in their neighborhoods. Also stressed was

# A R-E-A-L Movement

*Fred Williams is founder and executive director of the Cross Colors/Common Ground Foundation, a youth advocacy group based in the Watts section of Los Angeles. He was interviewed by* Sojourners *editor Jim Wallis shortly after the Gang Summit.*

The gang truce movement swelled because the young men were tired of killing each other. They knew that the only way to change it was to do something for themselves. LA is the gang capital of the world and when the young men there went public with the gang truce, it made others say, "Look, let's do the same thing here."

This country has never had young African Americans and Latinos come together on the premise that we are not here to shoot each other in the head. Our destinies are tied together; our future depends on each other. Our society has simply forgotten how valuable these young people are.

How do you translate a high-profile summit into a grassroots movement? It's about the day in and day out, people talking, people organizing—that's critical. You cannot just go into a city and claim to put together mass gang movements. It's going to turn and bite you.

The question is, How do we make it a R-E-A-L—not a R-E-E-L—movement? We need to stay about the business of organizing *for* young people instead of *around* them. If we step out of the organization of young people and into the capitalization of them, we've already lost the battle. ■

"Perseverance is more prevailing than violence; and many things which cannot be overcome when they are together, yield themselves up when taken little by little."
—Plutarch, Roman philosopher

the need to hold accountable neighborhood institutions such as churches, schools, media, businesses, and criminal justice agencies.

## THE POWER OF THE SPIRIT

THIS SUMMIT HAD moved beyond a "gang truce movement." There are 50,000 young people in Los Angeles gangs alone. The potential of such large numbers of people turning from self-destruction to community reconstruction is a source of great excitement.

Yet the forces and pressures arrayed against such a transformation are enormous. That sober reality was acknowledged in Kansas City and was evident in the weaknesses and limitations of the gathering itself. Post-summit tensions were inevitable and have since asserted themselves. How can an effective national network or organization be built when the daily intensity of local needs and crises demand the energy of the movement's best leaders? Can competition between strong leaders yield to the summit's practice of cooperation and promise of unity?

The truces in many cities are fragile but still holding. Can those truces be expanded to other neighborhoods and cities? There were no Asian gangs represented in Kansas City; that alliance may be problematic to make. Will there be a "truce" with law enforcement officials or even a partnership to end the violence that is still out of control in so many places?

Perhaps most important, can the resources be found to support the grassroots organizations that are so crucial to a lasting peace? Can the resources be found for the community-based economic development that alone can provide an alternative to the violence?

Perhaps it was the enormity of such questions that caused summit participants to speak so often of the need for spiritual power. I haven't been to a church conference in years where we prayed as much as we did at the Gang Summit. Every session opened and closed in prayer, and every time things got hot or conflictual (which was often) we would stop to pray.

I won't soon forget a moment, early on, when things might have fallen apart. In the midst of the shouting and chaos, a Baptist minister from Minneapolis named Jerry McAfee stepped to the microphone and sang Thomas Dorsey's gospel hymn "Precious Lord" with a voice like Luther Vandross. It quieted and settled the crowd, led to a prayer, and allowed us to begin again in a much better spirit.

From opening and closing prayer circles—with Christian, Muslim, Native American, Hebrew, English, and Spanish prayers—to the final worship service, the spiritual power of the summit was evident. Pastor Mac Charles Jones warned his congregation, "This service will be like no other you have ever experienced." The whole diverse congregation was the choir, singing with hearts full of thanksgiving and joy from the days just experienced.

> **"I**t's not just 'peacelovers' we need, but peacemakers—ones who are willing to stick their necks out and take risks."
>
> —Emmanuel Cleaver, mayor of Kansas City and United Methodist minister

Mac Charles Jones preached on the gospel story of the prodigal son. When the text said how the young man just "came to himself" in the hog pen, I thought of the gang members who have often told us how they "just woke up" and decided to stop killing each other. Tears and shouts of joy filled the whole sanctuary as young men came forward at the altar call. It felt like church that day—the way it's supposed to be, with people who hadn't been there in years.

THE GANG SUMMIT WAS a case study in conflict resolution. At St. Stephen's on Sunday afternoon, intense, profane shouting could be heard—not typical for a Baptist church. But would we rather have our young people shooting it out in the streets or shouting it out in our churches? What congregations, mosques, and community centers will open themselves up to these men and women who are looking for safe places to resolve their conflicts and begin the rebuilding process?

The hope of the Gang Summit will spread kid by kid, gang by gang, city by city. It will grow by patience, perseverance, exhausting work, and undeniable love. It won't be effectively spread through the media, but through hundreds of grassroots efforts and organizations that now desperately need our support.

As I was about to depart Kansas City, I thought about the men and women from the street gangs who had reached out their hands to one another and to us. Most of the rest of us at the summit came from the churches, despite the fact that our churches have mostly abandoned these angry youth. Yet here we were, all together.

Who will now take the hands of these brothers and sisters who have extended their hands to us? Who will covenant with these hopeful new leaders in forming partnerships to transform the urban landscape? Together we talked about a new day, and a new beginning. Now the work begins. ∎

*JIM WALLIS is editor of* Sojourners *magazine in Washington, D.C.*

## ORGANIZATIONS

**Barrios Unidos**, 313 Front St., Santa Cruz, CA 95060; (408) 457-8208.
**Common Ground**, c/o Markham Jr. High School, 650 E. 104th St., Los Angeles, CA 90002; (213) 249-4527.
**St. Stephen's Baptist Church**, 1414 Truman Road, Kansas City, MO 64106; (816) 842-6311.
**United for Peace, The City Inc.**, 1254 Russell Ave., Minneapolis, MN 35411; (612) 522-6552.

**BIBLE STUDY:** Luke 10:29-37.

**FURTHER READINGS:**
*Sojourners*, August 1993. Special Report on the Gang Summit.

## Questions:

■ *Jim Wallis referred to the Gang Summit as a "self-help" conference. How do self-esteem, self-respect, and self-control relate to the violence on our streets? How would you go about addressing these kinds of needs? How are these needs related to similar needs of your own?*

■ *Think about your response when you see a young man of color walking toward you on the street. What subtle messages do you give your children about "boys in the 'hood"?*

# OUT OF THE HOG PEN AND INTO COMMUNITY

*Finding ourselves at last.*

*by Mac Charles Jones*

*Rev. Mac Charles Jones, a* Sojourners *contributing editor, is pastor of St. Stephen's Baptist Church in Kansas City, Missouri, which hosted the Gang Summit in April 1993 (see "A Time to Heal, A Time to Build," page 26). This article is adapted from a sermon Jones preached at the closing worship of the summit.*

**"I had to force myself to bend my knees. And waves of shame and embarrassment would force me back up. For evil to bend its knees, admitting its guilt, to implore the forgiveness of God, is the hardest thing in the world."**
**—Malcolm X**

We need to understand what ought to be the response from the church, the community, and the world to this Gang Summit. One response to this summit has been from those in power who are afraid of an emerging new power and don't know what to do with it. It is the response of those who have exploited, robbed, and violated other communities, and as they see those communities no longer fighting each other and coming together, they are responding with fear.

I want to help folk understand that they don't have to be afraid. Yes, they're going to have to give up something. You can't steal, exploit, and create a negative situation, and then act like the victim is the only one to pay a price. You can't ask folk to give up their only means of survival and then act like you are not going to give up anything yourselves—but just applaud because they have given up the violence and the dope and all the stuff that you've been complaining about. Everybody's going to have to give up something.

THE STORY OF THE PRODIGAL SON from the gospel of Luke can help us here. In many ways it fits our own plight. It's a story of broken relationship. The younger boy in the text goes off to a far country; he leaves home. Before long he's lost ties with his community. His daddy doesn't know where he is. His mama can't find him. He's lost his identity. He doesn't know who he is anymore. Survival will sometimes do that to you. This young man, he lost himself.

Not only is he in a far country, but the money he had is lost. And the folk he thought he could trust, he couldn't trust. And the end result is that this young man is in a hog pen. The suggestion of the text is that he would have eaten the hog's food himself. That's a false identity. He has lost who he is.

*Rev. Mac Charles Jones speaks at the Gang Summit.*

My brothers and sisters, as you hear this text, I want you to understand that all of us have lost our identity. All of us have been fooling around in hog pens. All of us have acted out of character. That's what this culture does to us.

This culture makes people of color ashamed to be who they are. It makes those who are of European descent feel that they are beyond who they are. It creates walls that should not be. And we end up los-ing our basic identity. We start treating each other as objects rather than human beings. That's hog pen mentality.

When you violate another person, you're not violating something that has no feeling. You are violating God! And the violation is not just with a gun, or with something you put in folks' bodies. The violation can be done through a law in Congress. It can be done when folks refuse to pass deals that allow for jobs for young men and women who have nowhere else to turn. It can be done when we leave each other out here by ourselves, acting as if we don't care. We become like hogs in the hog pen.

The beauty of what happens in this text is based on the fact that this brother was a Jew. You have to understand how bad this is. In the Jewish community, the hog was the worst possible animal to be associated with. You don't fool around with no hogs. But this brother is in the pen with the hogs—about to eat its food!

Then a strange thing happened. The young man was born again. He didn't go to the church or synagogue to get born again. Right there in the hog pen he gained a new consciousness! The Bible says he came to himself.

At this summit, gang members didn't come to the church to be born again. Before they ever got here, they were talking about peace and justice— right there in the hog pen! They found themselves.

Now I've got to tell you, community, we've got to find ourselves. All of us have to come to a new awareness about our relationship to each other, because we've got our own hog pen. When we have our noses up, walking around with judgment on our faces, we're walking around in our own hog pen. We need to come to ourselves that we might be one.

WHAT WILL OUR response be when young folk who have decided to end the violence want a new beginning, and want to build a new vanguard movement? These young folk want to be a new voice for the whole community. They want to break down the barriers between each of our communities and join together with sisters and brothers learning to respect each other. What will our response be?

I want to tell you what the response in the Bible is. They had a party. They said get out the fatted calf, and they got out the best calf. They said I've got a robe that I've been saving for a royal guest. Royalty is about to show up! Get the best robe. Get the gold ring and put it on his finger. That was celebration, joy, and victory. Folks were ready to shout.

You have to understand, this was possible only because the father never gave up on his son. No matter how bad it looked, every morning the father was

> "**A**long the way of life, someone must have sense enough and morality enough to cut off the chain of hate. This can only be done by projecting the ethic of love to the center of our lives."
>
> —Martin Luther King Jr.

out of his bed, looking down the road to see if his son was on the way home. My brothers and sisters, we cannot give up on our daughters and sons. I don't care how bad other folk talk about you, don't you talk about yourselves like you don't know who you are. We've got to learn to have faith in one another.

The text says that the father saw his son at a distance. Remember, when he left home his belly was full, he had clean clothes, and he had money in his pocket. He looked like somebody. But now look at him. He's been in a hog pen. He's got nothing but heartache and pain. And yet his father saw him and knew him.

While he was yet in jail, he knew him. While he was yet on the streets, he knew him. While he yet had alcohol on his breath, he knew him. And he declared, I'm having a party, because he who was lost and she who was lost is now found. Glory hallelujah! It's party time. Go tell the ones who didn't believe it's party time.

Let me tell you about me. I wasn't always a preacher. I ran some streets myself. I know what it means to have to try to survive with the FBI after you. I've had some other folk after me, too. My mother used to wonder whether I would come home dead or alive.

But I want to tell you something. My mama and my daddy, they never forgot what I looked like. When I came home, they would be standing on the road waiting on me. One day I came down the aisle and said, "The Lord has called me to preach. I got to talk about justice for poor folks and about redeeming the streets."

You know what they did? They sang "Amazing Grace." He could have been dead today. But they just sang—amazing grace, how sweet the sound, that saved a wretch like me. I once was lost, but now we are found; was blind, but now we see. Through many dangers, toils, and snares, we have already come. T'was grace, God's grace, not my power, but God's grace, that brought me safely home.

I want to make an invitation now to those who want to lay down your colors—for those who want to find another way. I want you to know that from this day forward, a new thing is happening. This morning we are praying for peace and unity; for justice, love, and power. We are praying for a new community. We are praying for a party. Come to the altar, won't you?

I want some of the brothers to come and sit with those who come forward, because we want to understand what this means. After the party, the work has to begin. ∎

**BIBLE STUDY:** Luke 15:11-32.

> "I keep my ideals because in spite of everything, I still believe that people are really good at heart."
>
> —Anne Frank, German Nazi victim and diary author

## Questions:

■ *Jones states that we are all "fooling around in hog pens" as the prodigal son did. In what ways is this true in your life? How does thinking of yourself as above others put you in the hog pen?*

■ *Is it time for you to return home? Do you expect to be welcomed home with a feast? Do you welcome with a feast others who return home? What would it mean for you to "come to yourself" as the prodigal son did (Luke 15:17)?*

■ *Do you agree with Jones that this culture makes us act out of character? Or is it our character that makes us act up in this culture? What shapes our character?*

■ *How do you respond to "conversion" stories? What ones do you believe; what ones do you suspect? Do you notice anything about this?*

# OUR COMMON HOPE

*Healing the violence in our souls and in society.*

*by Alexie M. Torres*

We are a nation that has not known war in our land for more than 100 years, yet we remain a country that is held captive by the violence permeating our communities, our televisions, our homes, our very souls. Seeking sanity in the midst of this madness, we debate the rhetoric about how we must continue to "fight" and "struggle" for peace.

We analyze violence as the solitary expression of a troubled individual, a bad neighborhood, a different culture. But in these statements, themselves oxymorons, we fail to respond to our greater need to condition our hearts for peace.

I live and work in a community in New York's South Bronx that is covered in blood. On every street corner, the blood of the innocent is shed and cries out. These cries land on deafened ears, but Psalm 72:14 reminds me that their blood is precious in God's sight. The promise of my God is of another type of "blood covering"; it is the very blood of his son Jesus Christ, the only blood shed with redemptive value and the one I cling to fiercely (Hebrews 9:12).

We live in broken-down, callous environments that desensitize us to the reality that, as a nation with an abundance of things, we live in an absence of love, mercy, and compassion. Even in this environment where fear motivates, it remains true that "perfect love drives out all fear" (1 John 4:18), and it is obvious that we have yet to work on our ability to love.

There is an undeniable connection between poverty and crime, ignorance and violence. Acts of violence speak to the realities of our sin-seeped society, but if we listen closely we will hear them speak even more clearly to the condition of our souls. We have conditioned ourselves to avoid our emotions all together. Our pent-up pain, disappointment, and bitterness explode in violence that points to a much deeper anger, dissatisfaction, and emptiness. We can continue to blame society and march, fight, and legislate against all it has done to create these conditions, but when all is said and done, we need another response. We must respond with our souls.

Let us recognize our common guilt. As Christians, our greatest common denominator is that "all have sinned and fall short of the glory of God"

> "Acquire inner peace and a multitude will find their salvation near you."
> —Catherine de Hueck Doherty, Russian social welfare leader

(Romans 3:23). This means that we have all at once been both perpetrators as well as victims of violence, and, as such, we desperately need a Savior, one who understands our common anger and remains our common hope.

We are all the walking wounded. Whether you are with me in the South Bronx or a thousand miles away, my struggle is your struggle and it is a very intimate one. Henry Thoreau spoke a profound truth when he said that most people lead lives of "quiet desperation." We all long for peace. We have all been hurt.

As a child I was taught to pray for and believe in miracles, and I believe fiercely that we—our hands, our feet, our minds—are the greatest miracle of God's creation. We must be the miracle we pray for to end the violence. Our ever patient Creator awaits our response.

## FORGIVE OTHERS AND YOURSELF

WHAT IS THIS personal response we must proclaim? First we must learn to forgive. Every day we judge others' innocence or guilt and fail to practice mercy, compassion, and forgiveness. Forgiveness requires a stubborn commitment constantly to root out the bitterness that tries to plant itself in our hearts—because once it does, it is a tenacious weed that is hard to pull. To forgive is not to deny that we have been hurt, but to let go and consciously release others of what they have done to us. In so doing, we release ourselves.

Forgiveness is the lesson that is at the foundation of salvation. Christ died because we are all his broken and violent children, and in this great paradox of violence and redemption we find our strength to forgive.

## DO THE RIGHT THING THE RIGHT WAY

SECOND, I BELIEVE that we must take deliberate steps to be peacemakers and find peace in our souls. We have hearts full of a desire to right wrongs and injustices, but our motivation is not of peace. Many a revolutionary movement has died because it has been motivated by anger, hatred, and bitterness that, in the end, burns us out. When addressing violence, only the motivation of love sustains us. It brings us peace and perpetuates itself, making us stronger in the process.

Let us learn to sow love, hope, and joy by becoming deliberate and active peacemakers at home, with family and friends, and only then extending out into our communities and world. Then will we taste "the peace of God, which surpasses all understanding" (Philippians 4:7) that the apostle Paul knew even while surrounded by the violence of prison.

## TENDERNESS IN THE CONCRETE JUNGLE

WE MUST BELIEVE in the transforming power of love. There is little softness or gentleness on the hard streets where I live and even less tenderness and compassion. If we are to heal the violence in our souls, we must learn to treat each other and ourselves with love and gentleness. It is sad when we realize how rarely many of us are offered or allow ourselves to experience a tender or loving moment. We must learn to love even those who do not love us—embrace them—and like Christ, see them not as they are but as they can be.

## PRACTICE AUTHENTIC POWER

HEALING the violence in our souls requires us to remember what true power is. "Not by might, nor by power, but by my spirit" (Zechariah 4:6) is a concept of power that is totally contrary to that taught in our world. Power is money! Power is possessions! Power is prestige and position! By these standards, anyone who hears of the life of Jesus Christ and sees him hanging on the cross might think of defeat and powerlessness.

Yet we can look at the cross and see the victory there—the power of the omnipotent God of the universe who allowed his body to be beaten and destroyed so that we could live. True power does not come in the form of a Tech-9 assault rifle but in the humility of that kind of sacrifice.

## THE CHILDREN ARE WATCHING

FINALLY AND PERHAPS most important, let us heal the violence in our souls by reaching out to our children. Our success or failure in the domain of peace will be measured largely by our capacity to pass these truths on to our youth.

Our young people are truly children of war. They are surrounded by death and violence daily by media that present them with 200,000 acts of vio-

lence by the time they are 18 years old. They lose their educational, recreational, and artistic programs and their parks, libraries, and schools to regular budget cuts. We describe them as addicted, at risk, the "X" Generation. Defining them by their pathologies and not their potential, we forget that violent words can sting as much as a slap in the face. Our children grow up in a world where weakness is not taken lightly, so we should not be surprised at the hardness that is etched in their faces and at how merciless even their jokes can be.

We have developed many good methodologies and theories, but I am convinced that violence stops in a young person where love and compassion begin and where self-worth is opened up and fed with empowering challenges.

Children want alternatives to the violence in their souls as much as we do. We must teach children about God's great love. We must tell them that they are royalty, children of God, heirs to a kingdom, loved unconditionally, respected and full of dignity because, in Christ, they are full of his righteousness. In our society, our children have become "the stone that the builders rejected" (Matthew 21:42), but if we teach them well, they can become cornerstones of our search for peace.

As people of God, we have no business being in the business of reconciling, healing, and transforming our world with the seeds of violence still planted in our hearts. When we practice the healing of our souls we will marvel at the miracles and wondrous works of God transforming lives and breaking down strongholds—but first we must allow those in us to be broken. Wet with our tears, in the presence of the death that surrounds us, we have a greater hope that causes us to look inward and appreciate the life-giving and healing ways of our God. ∎

*ALEXIE M. TORRES is founder and executive director of Youth Ministries for Peace and Justice, 1372 Stratford, Bronx, NY 10472.*

*Robert Fox/Impact Visuals*

## Questions:

■ Do you think it is more difficult to talk about personal responsibility or social responsibility? Why?

■ Do you feel a split between those who recognize the structures that bind us and those who believe we are bound by our own personal choices? Is one side more "right" than the other?

■ How might your own inner healing contribute to the healing of violence in our society?

# TO GREET BROTHERS WITHOUT FEAR

## *The long process of healing after rape.*

*by Judith Floyd*

Pentecost is an anniversary time for me. Several years ago, I was assaulted and raped. It happened in the daytime, in my apartment complex, in another city. The man was a stranger to me. He was armed with a weapon. I feared for my life. I consider myself fortunate to have survived relatively unharmed physically. The emotional wounds, however, were devastating. It affected my life, and my faith journey as a Christian, in many ways.

Being raped changed my life—it changed me—more than anything I have experienced before or since. I saw myself change from a relatively independent, adventuresome woman to what felt like a raw bundle of nerves and fears. To be so emotionally fragile and out of control was extremely discomfiting. At times I questioned my sanity.

In some ways, the psychological aftermath has been as traumatic as the actual incident. The name for all that is post-traumatic stress syndrome.

I am not the same person I was before I was raped. Part of me died that day, never to be recovered, and I grieve the loss. But just as rape changed my life, so too has Jesus changed my life, as he has walked with me through that experience and its aftermath.

I have experienced much of the healing that comes with the passage of time, that comes with much inner work, that is mediated by the prayers and support of my community and friends, that comes from being in an environment where I could openly share and seek support as I needed to. But healing is a long process, and I am painfully aware of how far I have to go yet.

There is much unhealed. I expect I will be dealing with this, off and on, for the rest of my life—as I face my brokenness in relationships and my difficulty with trust and intimacy, as I struggle with my fears, as I work with issues of dependence and independence, as I react hypersensitively to other forms

**Lead me from death to life, from falsehood to truth**
**Lead me from despair to hope, from fear to trust**
**Lead me from hate to love, from war to peace**
**Let peace fill our hearts, our world, our universe.**
**—Satish Kumar, Indian writer**

of sexism, some more violent than others (street harassment, obscene telephone calls, the objectifying of women in media and advertising, and sexist language, to name a few trigger points).

Sometimes it seems overwhelming. But as I look back, I can say with thanksgiving that I have come a long way, that God has brought me a long way, and that gives me courage for the long journey ahead. I am confident that God will bring to completion the work of healing already begun.

AS A CHRISTIAN, I BELIEVE in the redemptive value of suffering. That is not to say I believe God wills us to suffer. I do not believe God willed me to be raped. Nor do I believe I did anything to provoke it. It was an unwarranted act of violence. But I believe in God's ability to redeem our suffering. That has been my experience. God has taken my suffering and used it to work good in my life. In many ways, I consider myself a better person for it.

I am more open and vulnerable now. I know my need for other people and for community. I am emotionally healthier for what I have worked through. I am also a more compassionate person because of what I have suffered.

I am a better health-care provider for it, as a nurse practitioner working primarily with women, many of whom have experienced much hardship and trauma in their lives, whether they grew up in the inner city or have recently arrived as refugees from Central America. This experience calls me to stand in solidarity with women (and men and children) throughout the world who have suffered much, and continue to suffer much, from oppression, injustice, and violence. I share in their suffering, and in their hope for a better future.

Being raped by a black man in a way sensitized me to the rape of a people. I know no better way to relate to what has been done to African Americans, and Native Americans and their lands, by my ancestors and contemporaries. While I continue to struggle with my fears (one of the negative effects of my experience), I am also more sensitive now to the other side of the story (one of the positive effects of my experience). Racial reconciliation has become a personal issue.

I am certainly stronger in my faith because of what I have gone through. My neediness has caused me to reach out to God, and for God's grace, as I otherwise would never have done. I am stronger in my faith; I have a stronger sense of God-with-me; and I am learning to share that with others.

I do not know what my life would have been like if I had never been raped. "What ifs" are futile. It happened, and it cannot be undone. It is part of my life history that I have to live with. I have dealt with it the best I could, and I have grown tremendously in the process.

I hope I never have to go through anything like that again. I hope no one does. But I have no regrets for the growth I have experienced through it all. I give thanks to God for all the good that has been worked in my life, and I hope through my life to touch others, as a result of what I have been through. My suffering has been amply redeemed, and I trust that will be true for the suffering yet to come as I continue this journey.

THE FIRST FEW YEARS AFTER I was raped, I was plagued by nightmares; I couldn't sleep with my back to the door (it was too vulnerable a position); I was "on edge" all the time; the world seemed a frightening and threatening place. I was angry at God. In my search to find meaning in my suffering, I had found no satisfactory answers. The questions foremost in my mind were, Why me? and, Where were you when I needed you?

One of the ways Jesus has touched me has been through dreams. I had been in Sojourners Community only about a year when I had a dream that I was raped again and again, repeatedly.

I woke up crying, trembling, frightened (as I frequently awoke from my dreams during that period of my life). But I was soon comforted, because I was given an understanding that I was experiencing the Stations of the Cross.

That dream was a significant turning point in my healing process. It was the first time I knew (really knew in the depths of my being) that Jesus was with me in my suffering, that Jesus had actually taken on and experienced my rape with me.

It cut through my anger and alienation and self-pity to turn around my question from, Why me? to, Why not me? or, Who am I to consider myself immune to such suffering? It helped me to find meaning in what I had experienced. To know that Jesus so identified with me in my suffering in turn enabled me to identify with Jesus in his suffering, and to identify Jesus in the poor, the oppressed, the suffering of this day and age, in a way I had not been able to before. That one dream has profoundly shaped my life.

I also have a dream for the future that shapes my life. I dream that someday I will be able to walk down any street in any neighborhood in any city, at any hour of the day or night, and encounter any man (whether he is alone or in the company of other men) by looking him in the eye and calling him "brother"—without fear, without guardedness, without threat to my safety—with only mutual good will.

I long for that day. But I can't get there alone. I need your help. Breaking the silence is an important step in the process of making that dream a reality for us all.

It is only as we come out in the open—with our experiences, with our pain, with our fears, with our outrage, with our hopes, acknowledging the obstacles in the way—it is only as we come together as people of God that we can truly open ourselves to God's spirit. And it is the Spirit that can fill us, empower us, use us as she will to make this world a better place for us all.

Holy Spirit, come. ∎

*JUDITH FLOYD was a longtime member of Sojourners Community and a nurse practitioner in Washington, D.C., at the time she wrote this article. She now makes harps and other crafts in a home studio in the Shenandoah Valley of Virginia.*

**If** a woman makes an act of power, she's created something like a work of art. It changes her forever. It gives her new vision on this mother earth, teaches her to see. Teaches her to know what she feels and teaches her to feel what she knows. When that happens, she can re-create herself.

**—Agnes Whistling Elk**
**Cree medicine woman**

"There never was a war that wasn't inward. I must fight 'til I have conquered in myself what causes war."
**—Marianne Moore, American poet**

## Questions:

■ *Is vulnerability truly a path toward finding the love and encouragement of God? Does such deep pain also lead people away from God? What steps of empowerment are necessary to open oneself to that path?*

■ *What do you believe is God's role in human suffering? Does God will suffering? How does Floyd's explanation of "redemptive suffering" fit with your view of the role of suffering and painful experiences? How have you grown through your experiences of struggle?*

■ *As women, do you feel threatened by men when you encounter them in situations in which you are (potentially) vulnerable? As men, do you feel that women view you as a threat? What effects does this have on your relationships?*

# NO SYMPATHY REQUIRED

*Why I live in the city.*

*by Karen Lattea*

> "The first thing to be disrupted by our commitment to non-violence will not be our system, but our own lives."
>
> —Jim Douglass, author and peace activist

## QUESTIONS:

■ *Where do we place our security? Is it in the police and military? In the government? In the suburbs? Where would you like to find your security?*

■ *It has been well documented that the massive flight of middle-class families to the suburbs is a major cause of crime and blight in the inner cities. How does this exodus from the cities affect those people who still live there? What implications does it have for those in the suburbs?*

■ *Why do you live where you live? Do your principles affect your decisions? What practical obstacles do we face in living up to our ideals? Do our ideals conflict at times?*

When I tell people I live in Washington, D.C., a common reply is, "I'm sorry to hear that." When a former D.C. paramedic discovered which neighborhood I live in, he didn't bother with condolences, he just told me I was "crazy." Friends responding to my Christmas letter about my experiences in the city wrote back words of comfort. All this has me wondering: Is a decision to live in the city cause for sympathy these days?

Indeed, violence rears its ugly head often on these streets, usually under cover of darkness, and that's what people hear about. And yet neighbors persist in greeting one another, quietly fighting back the fear behind the headlines. Vulnerability and grace walk hand in hand.

Why do I live in the city? Am I just "asking for trouble," as some say? Can I talk about my everyday experiences without promoting the very fear and judgment I seek to dispel?

I live in the city to be a witness against violence and injustice, and to experience firsthand its human and structural dynamics. When I stand in long lines at the few grocery stores, where prices are higher than in the suburbs and the food is lower quality, I understand demoralization; when I allow encounters with human tragedy to become part of my prayer life, rather than denying they exist, I understand the paradox of faith as my trust in God deepens. Meanwhile, I have the opportunity to share the satisfaction of organized neighbors who finally closed the crack house around the corner, and I am challenged when one of them offers assistance to those displaced—the same people who had kept him up nights for so long.

I've adopted some protections, or compromises, to minimize the real risks in my neighborhood. I don't live alone, I own a car, I walk at night only in groups, and, most important, I know my neighbors. On days when I'm feeling particularly vulnerable to street harassment, I avoid walking. If I have to park a few blocks away from home late at night, I wake up my housemate to walk with me. If requested, I call friends and family who live elsewhere to let them know I've arrived safely.

At the same time, I take steps to fight my fears, maintain my independence, and encounter the benefits of city life. I know the stakes of this balance are high. I've watched the struggle of friends who were robbed or assaulted, either their home or their person, as they try to overcome the violation. Some do and stay—some don't and move away.

Community and faith are my anchors here. When one of our members was mugged just a few hundred feet ahead of a group of us walking home from a meeting (at which the topic was how we can respond to violence in our neighborhood!), we immediately employed the ideas just spoken: We yelled at the guys who committed the crime, chasing them off our block, we put up fliers announcing that a mugging had occurred, and we became a little more determined and prayerful.

> Peace and love are always alive in us, but we are not always alive to peace and love.
>
> —Julian of Norwich

I live in the city by choice and calling. Everyday there are compromises and blessings, but I focus on the latter—the crossing guards who make children their priority every morning and afternoon, the guys hanging out on the corner who notice if I haven't been by lately, the diversity of residents living side by side in just one block.

These are the things that sustain me. Sympathy is not required. ■

*KAREN LATTEA is managing editor of* Sojourners *magazine and a member of Sojourners Community in Washington, D.C.*

# THE HIGH STANDARDS OF NONVIOLENCE

## *Strategies for self-defense.*

*Martha J. Langelan is a self-defense trainer, economist, and former vice president of the Washington, D.C. Rape Crisis Center. She is the author of* Back Off! How to Confront and Stop Sexual Harassment and Harassers *(Simon & Schuster, 1993) and recently offered workshops in self-defense at the Sojourners Neighborhood Center in D.C. Langelan was interviewed by* Sojourners' *assistant editor Julie Polter.*

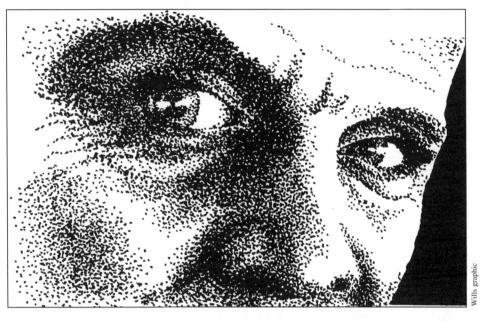

Wills graphic

**Polter:** Is nonviolence a realistic alternative in urban America? Often the choices are very polarized: Either carry a gun or be prepared some other way to deter your attackers, or stay out of the city or totally off the streets. What are our options, from your point of view as a self-defense trainer?

**Langelan:** I look at it in terms of how we humanize our community. In all my defense classes, I tell people, "Don't carry a gun. Don't have a gun in the house." I think that's absolutely the wrong direction. The best weapon is your brain, your voice, and your neighbors—not heavy armament.

On a philosophical level, the purpose of any feminist self-defense is not to stomp your opponent to the ground. It's not about revenge. It's not even about venting anger. It's about the effect of intervening at the earliest possible stages and stopping aggression with the minimum amount of force. Basically, the principles of feminist self-defense set some boundaries on how one responds to violence without giving vent to one's own rage. It's a very principled approach to self-defense.

A lot of the work I do is really prevention and awareness. Because there's so much in our society that isolates people, one of the first steps I advocate

for anyone working to make his or her neighborhood safer is to walk around and talk to people. Get to know names, say hello. Begin to build community one person at a time.

What makes a neighborhood work on every level is connection. Talk to people on the street, including the street people. We have stereotypes of homeless people as dangerous and, in fact, a few are. But the vast majority aren't. We've had a couple of incidents where homeless people actually intervened to stop sexual assaults. People are much more likely to intervene and keep an eye out for each other if they know each other. The neighborhood includes everybody.

The observation circle is an exercise we teach in self-defense classes. It involves drawing an imaginary circle, about 20 feet around you in every direction, and noticing three things you could identify about every person who moves within that circle. It's not a hostile glare, it's just attentive. We do this weird psychological thing where we think if we don't look at the other person they won't see us. But actually we look more vulnerable and out of place when we do that.

I recommend walking down the street being

very observant, nodding and saying "hello" to the person you are passing. It doesn't require a lot of interaction, but it's very different from the kind of isolated scurrying down the street that we adopt in urban areas.

This is the first step to starting to connect in your neighborhood. When you make eye contact with people, even briefly, it is humanizing, rather than dehumanizing. Just nodding and looking at somebody in the face is a way to begin connecting.

This also helps to cut down on street harassment. While walking down the street looking at people attentively, I've often had the experience of seeing them open their mouth to start yelling, but then close their mouth because I'm not looking like a victim, I'm looking like a neighbor. It's really interesting. It doesn't prevent harassment 100 percent of the time, but it does help.

I recommend that my classes do a walking tour on a nice afternoon with two or three people. Find out what's behind that hedge or what's down that alley. Look for safe places where you could run if you needed help. Find out who's around. Who would hear you if you yelled? Think about it in terms of knowing all of your options ahead of time. It's not paranoid to do this, it will give you extra time to react quickly if you need to. Know what resources you have. Thinking ahead of time about what you would do makes everybody safer.

**Polter:** It seems that the biggest part of feeling some level of safety in the city is a mental game.

**Langelan:** To rely on your observation skills, your knowledge of the neighborhood, and your neighbors is smarter than having any amount of heavy artillery. Most successful interventions use these tools. I joke in class about how your voice and your brain are your two top weapons, ahead of guns, knives, fists, feet, elbows, or anything else. You might use all of those at some point, but if you use your brain and your voice, you reduce the need to use all the rest.

It's important to understand how much power we do have. Older women have wonderful power, though our society defines them as powerless and invisible. I have seen women in their 70s or 80s bust up street fights with adolescent males by using their best mother or grandmother voice, saying, "Johnny, you stop that right now!" That's using your voice as a weapon. It's amaz-

ing. The authority of the older woman—the voice of a mother—is a very powerful tool.

Being willing to intervene is important, too. Anybody can do this. Little kids, people in wheelchairs, and people in their 90s can do it. One of the safest ways to intervene is from a distance, using your voice as a tool. I have busted up all kinds of situations on the streets by standing 30 or 40 feet away and yelling, "I see you. Stop hitting her! Leave that woman alone right now!"

You're trying to establish visibility and accountability. It's a mechanism that suddenly gives the victim an ally—though the ally may be 40 feet away or five stories up. It's important to disrupt the power dynamics between the aggressor and the victim by interposing a new element. There's an intervener now and the violent behavior has become visible. Someone is there saying, "This is going to stop."

I would encourage everybody to be alert; you have to notice what's going on before you can intervene. Think about what to say and how to say it. You can practice a little bit in the privacy of your home. How would it sound to hear those words coming out of your mouth in that kind of tone? Can you imagine doing that?

**Polter:** For myself, as a good Midwestern woman, I was not raised to speak up. We are conditioned that it's impolite to give commands or talk about the behavior of someone we don't know. That can trip us up even while somebody's getting hurt.

**Langelan:** It's not just the fear, it's cultural conditioning. Women in particular are socialized not to give commands, especially to an adult male. We'll think nothing of telling 6-year-olds what to do, but it's very rare for women to use commands with an adult male.

What you say and how you say it makes an enormous amount of difference. Yelling back obscenities or challenging his manhood will escalate the situation real fast. That's aggression. Nonviolence is based on respect. When you yell something like "Stop harassing women!" or "Let go right now," you're saying to somebody that you expect him to be a better human than he's being at the moment. You're holding him to a higher standard.

Part of why it works is the shock value of a direct command. Most aggressors think they know what's going to happen next. But when you don't respond in any of the predictable ways, the assailant feels at a loss. This means not doing the three traditional responses:

1. Pretend it's not happening. We are all dehumanized when we turn our backs without doing

## ORGANIZATIONS

**Washington Peace Center**
2111 Florida Ave. NW
Washington, DC 20008
(202) 234-2000

**Children's Creative
Response to Conflict**
7710 Carroll Ave.
Takoma Park, MD 20912
(301) 270-1005

**Training Center
Workshops**
4719 Springfield Ave.
Philadelphia, PA 19143
(215) 729-1910

*Also check out self-defense
courses offered by local
YWCAs, aikido or judo martial arts centers, or rape
crisis centers.*

something. Besides, it doesn't help the victim.

2. Get angry and scream abuse, obscenities, and go in swinging. That's very aggressive and almost without exception will escalate the situation. Aggressors are familiar with aggression and know how to respond to it. The response to aggression is more aggression and that's really dangerous.

3. Leave town, lock yourself in your house, or only go out with other people in broad daylight. What we lose then is the richness of life, the ability to be surprised. One of the joys of living in the city is that unexpected things happen. You make friendships that you would never have made across cultural, age, race, gender, and ethnic boundaries—the richness of that makes cities wonderful. Running away impoverishes us all.

**Polter:** But guns are everywhere. What do you advise when people are armed?

**Langelan:** Let's take an example of a street mugging, when someone pulls a gun and points it at you. At that moment you need to stay very calm and move slow and easy. Understand that you are dealing with a kid who's got a gun because he's scared and the gun makes him (or her) feel powerful and respected. You may need to hand him your wallet—that's just practical. But I want to come at it from a deeper level.

Thinking about the kid's need for respect at the moment of a street robbery is one of the useful ways to stay calm and not vent your anger at what he is doing. If you treat this kid with respect and speak in a calm tone of voice, rather than with anger, you are actually likely to de-escalate the level of tension.

One caveat: If you see somebody on PCP or crack, you need to steer clear because that person is unpredictable and may be violent. Also, be responsible about isolating the danger and keeping other people away from him. That's part of community responsibility.

It all comes down to living where you live in a responsible way. Take responsibility for the dynamics on the street and in your neighborhood. Do what you can everyday. Take time to sit on a park bench and talk to people. Call people to account when their behavior falls below a basic human standard.

You can change the tone of a block. Everybody's conscious of how other people's power affects them, but we don't think about how much power we have to affect other people. One of the things I see happen in self-defense classes is that people start claiming their power. Not just the power

> ## "Nonviolent resistance avoids not only external physical violence, but internal violence of spirit."
> —Martin Luther King Jr.

to get out of a choke hold or stop somebody who's coming after you physically, but the power psychologically to say, "I live here, I belong here. And I'm going to make it better."

Creative peacekeeping is intervening in a way that brings people back to their humanity. I have busted up incipient violence at marches by asking the guy who's about to slug somebody where the nearest restroom is. Almost anything can break up the energy flow and make something else happen instead. That means not acting like the victim yourself. It also means giving the aggressor a good alternative, making him aware that he has a choice at that moment, and nudging him to make the right one. We all have more power than we think we do.

We think of basic human needs as being food, water, clothing, shelter. But more fundamental than any of those is respect. So much violence is committed to enforce respect and so much violence is produced by lack of respect, whether it's racism or sexism. People dehumanize themselves when they commit violence, but there are ways stop it. I truly believe that. I am more optimistic now than I was 20 years ago.

I want to talk a little about language. When women fight back against a rapist and win, we never hear that. We hear about the terrible, horrible, mutilation killings—but we never hear about success stories. It's important that we tell each other! A 9-year-old who took one of my classes got jumped by two high school boys in an alley, and she fought them both off using these techniques. Instead of having a traumatized, raped 9-year-old, we have a 9-year-old with a sense of power, who's not helpless or a victim. That's going to stay with her forever!

When a woman fights off her attacker, something wonderful has happened. She responded out of her skills, her courage, and her resources in a way that stopped a violent attack. We ought to celebrate.

People do courageous, resourceful, smart, creative things all the time. When people stop an attack, we say "nothing happened." But something did happen. What happened was amazing and wonderful—human beings at their best, instead of their worst. ∎

### FURTHER READING

**Back Off! How to Confront and Stop Sexual Harassment and Harassers**. By Martha J. Langalen. Simon & Schuster, 1993.

**You Can't Kill the Spirit.** By Pam McAllister. New Society Publishers, 1988.

**This River of Courage: Generations of Women's Resistance in Action.** By Pam McAllister. New Society Publishers, 1991.

**We Are All a Part of One Another: A Barbara Deming Reader.** Edited by Jane Meyerding. New Society Publishers, 1984.

### Questions:

■ *What are your feelings about self-defense courses, nonviolent or otherwise? Does the Christian ethic of love conflict with the notion of being "cautious" or "prepared"?*

■ *Many believe that the only way to defend ourselves is with a gun. Do weapons truly make us more secure? Name some effective ways of protecting yourself that do not include arms.*

■ *What are some of the steps you can take in your neighborhood to be more safe? Do these measures serve to build up your community network or do they further isolate person from person?*

# 'THE THINGS THAT MAKES FOR PEACE'

## *Churches in solidarity with street youth.*

*by Jean Sindab*

It was a shining moment...for the church, for racial solidarity, for living out a Christian witness, for affirming the human community. It occurred as 800 pastors, lay persons, and street youth (gang members) came together at SCUPE's 1994 Urban Congress to discuss problems of economic and environmental justice, gang violence, homelessness, and racism.

The week generated the kind of excitement and controversy typical during social justice discussions within church settings. Not everyone felt comfortable with gang members because they were new to the mix. But it was important that these street youth be invited to tell their own story and issue their own challenge to the churches.

During the conference, Odies, one of the street youth, went for a walk. He met and befriended a homeless man, inviting him back to the hotel for a meal. Odies had attended the session on homelessness and violence. Perhaps it was the stories he heard in that session that drew him to his new friend and his desire to help him.

Hotel employees, however, were not so inclined. They were willing to let in cleaned-up homeless people to tell their story, but not this unkempt, dirty fellow. Despite Odies' explanations and entreaties, they ordered the man out.

Upset, Odies insisted the man had a right to stay as his guest. When hotel staff called security, Odies became furious. Security officers called the police, asking them to remove Odies and his new friend.

Odies, a very big and very black man, personifies the fear of America today on issues of crime and violence. Four squad cars responded to the hotel call. By then Odies was mad, frustrated, and more than a little confused. He understood in his previous encounters with police that there may have been some suspicion of wrongdoing. But here he was simply trying to feed a hungry, homeless man—

> **"I don't think any one event, or any one day, or any one action, or any one confrontation wins or loses a battle. You keep that in mind and be practical about it."**
> **—César Chávez**

what was the crime in that?—and he a legitimate participant of a church meeting at that!

The police pulled their clubs and stepped toward Odies. His intended act of kindness had degenerated into a full-blown crisis.

In another part of the hotel, the closing worship was in full swing. Participants were giving praises for the blessings of the week. Someone rushed to alert the convener, David Frenchak, that there was a major confrontation taking place in the lobby. Hurriedly he left the service, rushing into the lobby just in time to see the police moving toward Odies with raised billy clubs. Then came the moment of grace.

David, a middle-aged white man, put himself between Odies and the police. He announced in a strong, unwavering voice, "You will have to go through me to get to him. And if you touch either one of us, 500 people will be in this lobby in five seconds." The police backed off. The homeless man slipped out during the ensuing melee, probably feeling that one meal was not worth all of this.

Odies the gang member and David the intervener were left standing in the lobby face to face. For both it was a transformative moment.

The conference came alive in the person of David Frenchak. He brought a whole new meaning to the phrase "standing in solidarity with the oppressed." He now knows in a powerful way what we are called to as people of faith. Odies, perhaps for the first time in his life, saw someone he regarded as a power figure step into a new place as a fellow struggler. Most important, he witnessed the churches' commitment to support youth as they attempt to transform their lives.

## A TRANSFORMATIVE PATH

DAVE MADE REAL THE promise of those who sit around a new table in the ecumenical movement: a network called "The Things That Make for Peace: The Churches' Anti-Violence Action Network."

*Continued on Page 42*

# Creating Viable Options

Many nonviolent activists believe that violence occurs when creativity is lacking. The use of violence is the result of a person choosing the simplest option from a short list of alternatives. When individuals choose violence in difficult situations, they are usually treating their victim in the way they themselves are used to being treated.

Creativity is the opposite of the destructiveness of violence. Artistic ventures are one example of how young people can develop an outlet for their energies, while at the same time increasing the number of opportunities available to them. The arts, music, sports, and similar activities have often provided the means for young people to step out of the cycles of violence that can control their lives.

The creative energies of urban youth need to be transformed into what they often need most: a legitimate means of supporting themselves and providing for their families. Creative outlets alone cannot provide a long-term solution for the problems that many urban youth face. Yet combined with the knowledge of those who have business experience—and capital— young people are capable of the powerful act of creating small (or even large) businesses and organizations that not only provide them with their own means of support, but also offer a positive contribution to the world.

The tags—or graffiti—of young people, visible on the walls of every American city and town, are an example of their creativity. Yet, without guidance, artistic young people risk jail time, the ire of property owners, and the annoyance of other citizens just for the opportunity to express themselves and their talents in public.

"Why should they be doing it for free when they could be getting paid for it?" asked Otilio Quintero, assistant director at Santa Cruz Barrios Unidos. An important part of Barrios Unidos' work to provide alternatives for Latino youth has been the development of economic initiatives that are capable of turning the lives of young people around. The group recruits local taggers to create art for silk-screen T-shirt production. The young people earn money and learn job-readiness skills.

"By teaching kids how to do silk-screening and work with their art, we are giving them a skill that they could turn around and get a job with somewhere else," said Manuel Martinez, who coordinates Barrios Unidos' silk-screen program. The vivid T-shirts also further the outreach efforts of the group in the community.

JOBSTARTS INC. is another group that works to solve some of the problems of violence through economic development. The church-based community development organization works with gang-affected families in South Central Los Angeles to improve economic stability and self-reliance through work. JobStarts Inc. offers "a hand up, not a handout to many broken people in the community."

Father Greg Boyle, a Jesuit priest at Delores Mission Church in East Los Angeles, has become a local hero because of his work with youth-at-risk. One of the most tangible ministries he helped to initiate is the Jobs for a Future program. Jobs for a Future organizes places for young people to work at the church or in the local community, with the ministry—if local businesses are unable—footing the bill for their salaries. With a long waiting list for positions, Boyle's program dispels the myth that gang-related youth prefer dealing drugs to honest work.

One of the most innovative projects of the Delores Mission is Homeboy Tortillas, a small tortilla-making company in LA's oldest marketplace. Homeboy Tortillas employs members of rival gangs to make tortillas (and money), while making peace.

Tony Campolo's UrbanPromise ministry in Camden, New Jersey, offers several initiatives to help young people break the cycle of poverty and violence in their lives. One of their programs focuses on developing youth leaders by providing them with summer employment and a positive environment in which to nurture their skills. Hundreds of young people apply each summer for one of the 70 positions offered by UrbanPromise. Those hired then receive on-going training and are exposed to various educational and career opportunities, with the belief that each young person should have options when it comes to deciding what direction their lives will take.

The groups listed above represent just a few of the many organizations that are using local economic development to quell the tide of violence in their communities. Equally important are the connections between the young people in the streets and the local business community— directing all of the human and financial resources of a neighborhood toward the work of life and hope. It can be as complex as building a local revenue-generating enterprise from the ground up, or as simple as area businesses paying young people to clean up around the neighborhood. Just do it!

—**Aaron Gallegos**

**The creative energies of urban youth need to be transformed into what often they need most: a legitimate means of supporting themselves and providing for their families.**

## Study Question

■ *America's churches have an investment portfolio that is estimated to be about $34 billion. Can you name ways that this money is currently being invested? Are there ways it could be invested that might have an impact on lessening violence in our society?*

This network emerged from the churches' commitment to follow up on the Urban Peace and Justice Summit (the "Gang Summit") of April 1993, which brought together 160 gang leaders and church observers. During a three-day meeting, a truce agreement was forged between some of the most notorious gang leaders in urban America.

After the summit, church representatives helped with fund raising, facilitating dialogue to keep the truce agreement moving forward, and mobilizing denominations to become involved. Many of the NCCC member churches—together with evangelicals (including World Vision), Roman Catholics (including Campaign for Human Development), and urban activists—committed to build a partnership with pastors who have established a youth anti-violence ministry.

The network has set five key objectives:

1) articulating a Christian vision of bringing about community peace and justice,

2) articulating theologically the importance of youth and anti-violence work,

3) serving as a catalyst to mobilize human and financial resources to support local anti-violence efforts,

4) providing technical advice and assistance to youth, and

5) bringing new definitions to old words, concepts, and programs of the church; for example, applying peace, disarmament, and sanctuary to the domestic urban situation.

The network has two task forces: economic development and peace. In meetings, the needs of the cities are articulated by the pastors and youth, and the resource people from the churches respond to them. Tasks include:

1) maintaining and expanding urban peace truces.

2) providing forums and creating opportunities for young folk to tell their stories to each other and to congregations.

3) establishing alternative economic opportunities.

4) securing additional church support for local anti-violence initiatives.

At the Gang Summit and all subsequent encounters with street youth and their supporters, the emphasis has been on creating economic alternatives to the underground drug economy driving so much of the crime and violence in urban America. The network has economic development experts exploring the specifics of generating entrepreneurship, jobs, and training opportunities for youth.

Pastors and youth are involved in a variety of economic development activities: producing T-shirts, tie-dye clothing, and silk-screened posters; renovating housing and providing security services; purchasing and rehabilitating old houses and establishing apprenticeships; producing "cross-color" clothing, helping to reduce violence, and working on urban gardens to sell produce at farmers markets; and starting businesses to provide services in beauty culture, hair and nails, child care, and elderly care.

Crime and violence are creating fear and anger throughout the United States. The lack of jobs and urban investment, as well as the reality of racism, exacerbate this predicament. The situation's seriousness calls for the churches to assume new forms and adjust their processes and structures to meet new needs and challenges.

The pastors involved in this network walk the pain-riddled streets, go into drug houses, and visit the courts, schools, hospitals, and funeral homes. They are teaching and preaching. They are reaching out, bringing in, breaking stereotypes of the perception of the church, attending to needs, and, most of all, giving love and assurance.

PASTORS IN THE NETWORK share the gospel of love to save our youth. This is not a two-hour-a-week ministry; it requires 24 hours each day, seven days each week. They are bringing these young people back from the fringes of society where they have been pushed. They deal with the tremendous personal and family problems and the responsibilities the young people bear. They guide them in strengthening their faith and trusting God's love to provide them with the fortitude to stay on the transformative path.

These young people are just discovering the power of God in their lives. One young man who is experiencing tremendous problems said, "It is really hard when you are trying to turn your life around, but I believe God saved me for a specific purpose. So, I have a mission to accomplish."

Can we help these young people in their mission? I believe so! It won't be easy, but we have no other choice. They are our future. We have to bring in more church partners and mobilize more local congregations to be involved.

We have to be just as strong as Dave Frenchak and be willing to stand with our young people in the tough places of life, to be an advocate for them and a friend to them, to confront the powers and principalities on their behalf. This is what our faith—our belief in Jesus Christ our Savior—should be all about: being doers of the Word, not just sayers. These are indeed the things that make for peace. ■

*JEAN SINDAB was program director of Environmental and Economic Justice/Hunger Concerns of the National Council of Churches of Christ. She died of cancer in January, 1996.*

## ORGANIZATIONS

• **SCUPE** (Seminary Consortium for Urban Pastoral Education), 200 N. Michigan Ave., Suite 502, Chicago, IL 60601-5909. (312) 726-1200.

• **National Council of Churches of Christ** (NCCC), 475 Riverside Drive, Room 572, New York, NY 10115. (212) 870-2298.

• **Community Renewal Society,** United Church of Christ, 332 South Michigan, Chicago, IL 60604. (312) 427-4830.

**BIBLE STUDY:** Luke 19:41-44

## Questions:

■ Read Odies' story again. What role did cultural-specific perceptions and understandings play? Can you see something similar happening at one of your church functions? How can we begin to reconstruct those perceptions to avoid such conflict?

■ Is police brutality an issue in your area? What are the relations between the police and the community? Is it different for different groups? How do race, class, and culture affect these relations and why?

■ Has anyone ever intervened for you in a threatening situation? Have you ever intervened for someone else? What goes through your mind as you choose to risk your own well-being to protect someone else?

# A CALL TO ACTION

## *A 10-point plan to mobilize churches.*

*This plan emerged from the Ten Point Coalition, a group of churches working in Boston's inner-city neighborhoods.*

The following 10-point proposal for city-wide church mobilization is born of the realities of our day-to-day work with the youth on the streets, in the crack houses, and in the courts and jails of this city. We seek to generate serious discussion regarding the specific ways the Christian community can bring the peace of God to the violent world of our youth.

We therefore call upon churches, church agencies, and the academic theological community throughout the city to consider, discuss, debate, and implement, singly or in collaboration, any one or more of the following proposals:

**1.** To establish four or five church cluster-collaborations that sponsor "Adopt a Gang" programs to organize and evangelize youth in gangs. Inner-city churches would serve as drop-in centers providing sanctuary for troubled youth.

**2.** To commission missionaries to serve as advocates for black and Latino juveniles in the courts. Such missionaries would work closely with probation officers, law enforcement officials, and youth street workers to assist at-risk youth and their families.

To convene summit meetings between school superintendents, principals of public middle and high schools, and black and Latino pastors to develop partnerships that will focus on the youth most at risk. We propose to do pastoral work with the most violent and troubled young people and their families. In our judgment this is a rational alternative to ill-conceived proposals to suspend the principle of due process.

**3.** To commission youth evangelists to do street-level one-on-one evangelism with youth involved in drug trafficking. These evangelists would also work to prepare these youth for participation in the economic life of the nation. Such work might include preparation for college, the development of legal revenue-generating enterprises, and the acquisition of trade skills and union membership.

**4.** To establish accountable community-based economic development projects that go beyond "market and state" visions of revenue generation. Such economic development initiatives will include community land trusts, micro-enterprise projects, worker cooperatives, community finance institutions, consumer cooperatives, and democratically run community development corporations.

**5.** To establish links between suburban and downtown churches and front-line ministries to provide spiritual, human resource, and material support.

**6.** To initiate and support neighborhood crime-watch programs within local church neighborhoods. If, for example, 200 churches covered the four corners surrounding their sites, 800 blocks would be safer.

**7.** To establish working relationships between local churches and community-based health centers to provide pastoral counseling for families during times of crisis. We also propose the initiation of abstinence-oriented educational programs focusing on the prevention of AIDS and sexually transmitted diseases.

**8.** To convene a working summit meeting for Christian black and Latino men in order to discuss the development of Christian brotherhoods that would provide rational alternatives to violent gang life. Such brotherhoods would also be charged with fostering responsibility to family and protecting houses of worship.

**9.** To establish rape crisis drop-in centers and services for battered women in churches. Counseling programs must be established for abusive men, particularly teen-agers and young adults.

**10.** To develop an aggressive black and Latino history curriculum, with an additional focus on the struggles of women and poor people. Such a curriculum could be taught in churches as a means of helping our youth to understand that the God of history has been and remains active in the lives of all peoples. ∎

**Principal authors:** *Jeffrey L. Brown, Union Baptist Church; Ray A. Hammond, Bethel African Methodist Episcopal Church; Eugene F. Rivers III, Azusa Christian Community; Susie Thomas, Mt. Olive Temple of Christ; Gilbert A. Thompson, New Covenant Christian Center; Bruce H. Wall, Dorchester Temple Baptist Church; Samuel C. Wood, Lord's Family African Methodist Episcopal Zion Church. Brown, Hammond, and Wood are members of the executive committee of the Ten Point Coalition.*

# 'WE'RE IN THE FORGIVING BUSINESS'

*Barrios Unidos' spiritual movement against gang violence.*

*by Aaron Gallegos*

Santa Cruz, California, isn't the type of community that one would expect to be struggling with gang-related violence. A small city on the Pacific coast, Santa Cruz draws tourists from all over Northern California to its beaches and boardwalk amusement park. The city also attracts students from around the state to attend the University of California at Santa Cruz. Once a slow-paced fishing town, Santa Cruz is now a center for radical politics and the arts, and abounds with organic food stores, theaters, funky coffeehouses and restaurants, and alternative bookstores.

But like many small cities in California, Santa Cruz is a place of drastic contrasts and wild contradictions. Unseen by most of the visitors—yet literally adjacent to the popular beach boardwalk—there exists a section of this small town that faces the big problems of the inner city: low-income housing projects with teen-age heroin addicts, youth who are at risk from gang-related violence, and families who struggle to put enough food on the table for their children. For many of the predominantly white residents and students in Santa Cruz, the life —*la vida loca*— of the barrios is a distant reality that they read about in the newspapers or see on television more often than face to face.

> **Then Peter came to Jesus and asked, "Lord, how many times shall I forgive my brother when he sins against me? Up to seven times?" Jesus answered, "I tell you, not seven times, but seventy times seven times."**
> **—Matthew 18:21-22**

Gangs in Santa Cruz County, which are made up almost exclusively of Latino youth, exist in a complex network of ever-changing alliances, subsets, and crews, each loosely connected with California's two major Latino gang alliances, Norteño and Sureño (Northern and Southern). The Norteño alliance, which identifies itself with the color red, is associated with the Nuestra Familia gang that started in 1965 in Soledad penitentiary. The Sureño alliance, which is connected to the Mexican Mafia, a gang that began in a California prison in 1958, claims the color blue. Sureños generally consider themselves to be Mexican nationals and usually speak Spanish.

In Santa Cruz County, the Norteño-allied gangs include Northside Watsonville (the Northsiders), which, with about 300 members in 10 subsets, is the largest and oldest gang in the county; City Hall, which broke off from the Northsiders in the 1970s; and Westside Santa Cruz, which is one of two multiracial county gangs. Sureño gangs include Poorside Watsonville, which is active mainly in the migrant farmworker camps and has about 100 members; Eastside Santa Cruz, which includes the Beach Flats barrio where many newly arrived immigrants to Santa Cruz live; and Villa San Carlos, which is active in the low-income housing projects of the same name and includes Latino, African-American, and white members.

Although these alliances and groupings are helpful to understand the gang structure in Santa Cruz County, one must be careful not to interpret them too strictly. The connections between the gangs and the young people in them are constantly in flux. In a *Santa Cruz Sentinel* report on area gangs, Henry Robles, a Watsonville gang investigator for the police, said, "A lot of Northsiders grew up here and have family ties with Poorsiders and City Hallers. They are cousins. We literally have family members killing family members."

MANY OF THE solutions to urban violence proposed by adults have focused on working to eradicate gangs from our society. But youth gangs won't go away until society works together with youth to address the issues that cause young people to join gangs in the first place.

Barrios Unidos in Santa Cruz is part of a growing movement of church people, community activists, educators, and ex-gang members who, instead of blaming young people for society's problems, are sticking with them to work in creative ways to end the violence. "The reason why these groups start in the first place is because a lot of the kids can't afford anything else," says Elizabeth Ayala of Barrios Unidos. "Gangs are the cheapest club they can afford. They start as a friendship kind of thing and one thing leads to another. I wouldn't even call them gangs unless they're doing criminal activities. Young kids really just want a place to fit in."

Otilio Quintero, the assistant director of Barrios Unidos, says the impetus that drives gang-related activity is "misdirected energy that we have to work to redirect in ways that are positive and creative rather than destructive."

Barrios Unidos, whose name means "United Neighborhoods," was founded in 1977 by Daniel "Nane" Alejandrez. It is the local manifestation of The National Coalition of Barrios Unidos, of which Nane is also a founder. A veteran of the Vietnam War and a former drug addict, Nane saw 14 of his relatives die in 10 years due to gang-related violence, including two of his three brothers. "After a while, you'd become callous to funerals," Nane told *The Good Times*, a Santa Cruz weekly. "I didn't know how to deal with the deaths of my heroes and mentors. When I lost them, it was like I lost a big part of myself."

When he nearly died from an overdose, Nane had a revelation and realized where his life was headed. "The Creator gave me a vision, a chance to see my brothers," Nane said, and he turned his life around and committed himself to the peace and survival of his community.

The success of Barrios Unidos is in part due to the fact that they teach from experience. Most of the staff members at Barrios Unidos came out of the barrios themselves and can show young people the consequences of their lifestyle. "Barrios Unidos

"**They have joined gangs, sold drugs, and, in some cases, inflicted pain on others. But they have also played baseball and gone on dates and shot marbles and kept diaries. For, despite all they have seen and done, they are—and we must constantly remind ourselves of this—still children.**"

**—preface to *There Are No Children Here*, by Alex Katlowitz, 1991**

Ella Seneres

# 'VIOLENCE AFFECTS EVERYONE'

*MaryLou Rangel, 37, has been involved in the gang peace movement since she was 14 years old. After drifting away for a while, she came back and now is Barrios Unidos' office manager and bookkeeper. She was interviewed by Aaron Gallegos in January 1995.*

Violence has been in my family for a long time. After my drug addiction, I returned to give back to the community. I've been clean for eight years now, and that makes me feel better about all the things I did when I wasn't clean. It's my way of giving back what I took away or what was taken away from me. Barrios Unidos has been my support system in more ways than one.

I always tell people that it's important to get involved in something that you believe in. Just give a little bit of yourself to the people out there. Violence doesn't care what color you are, how rich you are, or how poor you are—violence affects everyone. ■

teaches kids to have hope through people that have already been through the system—ex-gang members, ex-felons, people who know what is involved," says Manuel Martinez, a program coordinator. "The media glorify this gang stuff, but Barrios tells them what to expect."

"We are teaching the kids how to survive," says Elizabeth Ayala, "by being survivors ourselves. We didn't read any books on the topic."

THE WORK of Barrios Unidos draws on the spirit of indigenous traditions and, increasingly, that of the progressive church community. "The End Barrio Warfare movement is a spiritual movement to us," says Nane Alejandrez. "We have to be prepared spiritually in order to try to stop the violence. It's a long journey. If we don't have that, it is very easy to get lost in the daily madness and pain.

"For some time we have felt abandoned by the church on this issue, but in the last couple of years more people are seeing that the church has to be involved. This has given people in the movement hope that we are not out here alone.

"For us to say we have certain churches behind us is very new and very powerful. It's also good for the churches to be able to say that they are out on the streets—or at least that they are supporting people working in the streets. The business, education, and law enforcement communities once [ignored] us by saying we're just a bunch of hoodlums coming together. But with the church behind us, they can't write us off as easily."

The spiritual support of the Chicano community has both Christian and Native American roots. The burning of sage and sweetgrass recalls the purification and inspiration that are at the core of Barrios Unidos' work. The image of the Guadalupe brings to mind their motherly devotion to the community. Every Saturday night "sweats" are held by one of the group's spiritual mentors, Henry Dominguez, a veteran activist in both the Chicano and Native American movements.

"Going to the sweat lodge and having members of different congregations come to sweat with us helps us see what we need to go through to deal with the madness," says Nane. "There're a lot of differences between us, but when we go into the sweat lodge we care for each other and pray for peace and patience together. We pray for people to realize what we are trying to accomplish here.

"We had been taught to be ashamed of our indigenous culture. But we are finding out more about ourselves and our Indian background, and we are embracing that. We see that our grandfathers and grandmothers had a lot going for them and that we have gotten away from them while living in the cities."

The spiritual core of Barrios Unidos feeds the outer life of their work as well as the inner. "Spirituality, that's what keeps us going," says Frank Gonzalez, an organizer at Barrios Unidos. It is the force that makes it possible for them to go one

# 'WE HAVE TO PASS ON OUR HOPE'

step further than even they thought possible.

"We are in the forgiving business," says MaryLou Rangel, who works as the office manager of Barrios Unidos. "The forgiving business is easier said than done. Sometimes when a person comes here and wants to do right they'll be OK for a couple of weeks, then the street life gets to them. Our job is to keep our door open all the time for these people to come back. Everyone has their own pace. We are not here to judge people.

"It starts by working within yourself first. Before it can work with anyone else, you have to find peace with yourself," she says. "Nane has done a tremendous job of showing us how to be humble. It's not an easy thing to learn. We all have to have patience with everyone we come across."

BARRIOS UNIDOS' LATEST project is the César Chávez Institute for Social Change, a dream that has been 20 years in the making. The mission of the institute is to raise up community leaders in the tradition of César Chávez, Martin Luther King Jr., and Mahatma Gandhi—barrio warriors who through nonviolent action bring justice to their neighborhoods.

The institute is housed in a new office building in downtown Santa Cruz, along with Barrios Unidos' administrative offices. Its academies include a dance studio where young people learn Latino folk and popular dance styles, a silkscreen production facility, a computer training lab with online capacity, a small auditorium to hold community events and presentations, and a video studio where young people will produce their own videos with the assistance of Santa Cruz's community access cable network, with whom they share the building.

Knowing that it is easier to affect the lives of young people if they reach them before gangs do, Barrios Unidos also runs "kids clubs" in three locations: the low-income housing projects Villa San Carlos and Neary Lagoon, and in the Beach Flats barrio in Santa Cruz. In the kids club program, young people between the ages of 5 and 15 participate in recreational activities, arts and crafts programs, and peer support groups. By exposing children in the housing projects to activities and

*Elizabeth Ayala, 29, has been working with Barrios Unidos for eight years. As site coordinator, she oversees all of the organization's programs. Elizabeth also runs a group for young women in the Beach Flats barrio. She was interviewed by Aaron Gallegos in January 1995.*

I have family members that have been in and out of prison, getting shot at, and getting killed. By the time I was 13 years old, I already knew what gang violence was. I had a few scars. There was a lot of pressure growing up in that kind of environment. I got involved in Barrios Unidos because of what was taking place in my family. I thought that it would be good for me to try to help somebody.

I'm trying to give females skills in dealing with relationships. A lot of young women are getting into relationships and getting pregnant, and then the guys leave them and they end up on welfare as single parents. "You could be traveling around the country the way I am," I tell them. "But if you have kids at a young age, it's going to be tough."

We have to pass on our hope to the kids out there. Then they pass it on to other kids. I used to run an alcohol and drug prevention program in Beach Flats. Now, the kids that I worked with there are either in college or leading their own kids clubs here in the area. The kids that we work with have a lot to offer. You have to pass it on. ∎

lifestyles that they may never otherwise have access to, Barrios Unidos hopes to broaden their horizons and offer them alternatives to the lure of gangs that they face as they become teen-agers.

"We're teaching them to be leaders in the community," says Barrios Unidos' Frank Gonzalez, who works with young people in the Villa San Carlos housing project. Unlike other programs, Barrios Unidos makes a point of being with the kids fulltime, including weekends, nights, and holidays. These kids hear about the dangers and problems of gang-related life from the firsthand testimony of ex-bangers from Barrios Unidos, but many feel they have little choice about whether to get involved in local crews. Because they and their families live in a neighborhood that can at any time be attacked by members of another barrio, it is hard for them—when their love and loyalty are put on the line—not to join others in defending their own.

For older youth, Barrios Unidos runs programs that are focused on job skill development and the creation of small business enterprises. Manuel Martinez coordinates Barrios Unidos' silkscreen production program that channels the artistic skills of barrio youth into revenue-generating enterprises.

"Producing their art into T-shirts has given them self-esteem," says Manuel. "It gives them great joy to see that their art is actually worth something. By developing their skills, they could turn around and get a job silkscreening somewhere else."

Women have played a crucial role in Barrios Unidos since the organization started, with longtime activists Elizabeth Ayala, MaryLou Rangel, and Argelia Flores especially focusing on the experience of women. "Sometimes in our culture, the men tend to outvoice the women," said MaryLou Rangel. "But we are not here to stand behind them or in front of them, we are here to stand by them. We need them just as much as they need us.

"I wish a lot more women would get involved in the peace movement," she says. "The compassion that women bring to the organization is very important. Women bring a different view that can enlighten the men. The male and the female views really need to come hand in hand in order to move forward."

AFTER YEARS of not being trusted, Barrios Unidos now works with other Santa Cruz organizations to build greater support for their work in the community. "We work in collaboration with the parks and recreation department, and the police at times cooperate with us," says Elizabeth Ayala. "Although some of the kids might think we're snitching, collaboration means working together as

> "The future is not a result of choices among alternative paths offered by the present, but a place that is created. The paths are not to be found, but made, and the activity of making them changes both the maker and the destination."
>
> —John Schaar, author

equals. We try to work on those terms. If the adults can't get along, how can we go to the schools and tell the kids that they should?"

Through work with the city's Arts Council, they have gotten grants for murals and other projects that are geared toward incorporating barrio *cultura* into citywide projects. "We are getting more support now. Before we couldn't even go into the schools," says Elizabeth. "A lot of people were in denial that gang violence existed in the community. But now, they have seen the need for Barrios Unidos here."

Though Barrios Unidos is primarily a Latino-focused organization, they are working to bring more volunteers from different backgrounds into their work. "The kids really appreciate that," says Elizabeth Ayala.

"It's not only Chicanos and blacks killing each other," she says. "We have whites and Asians and all kinds of kids doing the drive-by shootings and everything else. We need to come together; it's the only way to do it. If you walk into this office with purple hair and green eyebrows we're not going to turn you away. It's not how you look, it's what you have to offer."

It is necessary for everyone—adults and young people, rich and poor—to look within themselves for change to begin. As writer and youth activist Luis Rodriguez wrote in *The Nation*, "We must recognize that our battle is with a society that fails to do all it can for young people—then lays the blame on them. It's tougher to walk these streets, to listen to young people, to respect them and help fight for their well-being. It's tougher to care." ∎

*Barrios Unidos has 13 chapters in California and more than a dozen others in states around the country. For more information contact Barrios Unidos, 313 Front St., Santa Cruz, CA 95060; (408) 457-8208.*

AARON GALLEGOS *is an assistant editor of* Sojourners *magazine.*

## FURTHER READING

**Always Running. La Vida Loca: Gang Days in L.A.** By Luis J. Rodriguez. Simon & Schuster, 1993.

**Crews: Gang Members Talk to Maria Hinojosa.** By Maria Hinojosa. Photographs by German Perez. Harcourt Brace & Co., 1995.

**Father Greg and the Homeboys: The Extraordinary Journey of Father Greg Boyle and His Work With the Latino Gangs of East L.A.** By Celeste Fremon. Hyperion, 1995.

**There Are No Children Here: The Story of Boys Growing Up in the Other America.** By Alex Katlowitz. Nan A. Talese/Doubleday, 1991.

**Questions:**

■ Nane Alejandrez talks about developing a callousness toward funerals and death. What have you become callous to? What in our society do you accept that is unacceptable? How does fatigue, jadedness, and cynicism erode your commitment to peace?

■ What personality strengths do you bring to ministry? Does your gender affect your approach? How do you interact with co-ministers who have different strengths or gifts?

■ What specific spiritual resources can your community of faith offer youth, especially those "at risk"?

■ How can your church "be in the forgiving business"? What does Matthew 18:21-22 mean for your life?

# TO BREAK THE CHAINS OF VIOLENCE

## Building community and self-esteem.

*The Break and Build coalition of Kansas City was formed by gang members who sought a different way to address the issues in their communities. Here, seven gang leaders define the violence they see in their community. Within their definitions are ideas about how they have pledged to continue working in their neighborhoods.*

*The following is excerpted from Break and Build's Problem Definition and Vision Statement. For more information, contact Operation Break and Build, 2000 E. 12th St., Kansas City, MO 64127; (816) 842-7080.* —**The Editors**

**Violence** to ourselves and our community is the best definition of the problem. This violence is manifested in the following ways:

**1. The violence of unemployment and lack of economic opportunity for those who live in our neighborhood.**

This situation creates the condition of poverty and lays the groundwork for the violence of poverty, hunger, disease, poor diet, family breakdown, and intense personal stress.

**2. The violence of stress both for the individual and within the community.**

Stress produces tension that is often manifested in acts of violence and conflict in the home and neighborhood. This stress over survival leads to a breakdown in relationships in the home and the neighborhood. Ultimately it leads to the death of many young people.

**3. The violence of low self-esteem, generated primarily by systemic racism and its antecedents of poverty and ignorance.**

This is the violence of internalized oppression of racism and sexism. It manifests itself in acts of

violence against others, in black-on-black (self-against-self) crime, and in violence against women. The insidious nature of this violence is manifest in the effort always to blame the victim for the violence they face.

**4. The violence between men and women.**

Domestic violence is brought on by the general attitude of sexism that pervades the culture, with its low value of women and the general condition of poverty. This violence is manifested in the home and in the day-to-day relationships between men and women. The issue of the use of women as sexual objects is of extreme importance and is a core dimension of this violence.

**5. The violence of the police force and the courts.**

These systems commit acts of violence against urban youth, especially young black men, as they first demonize them and then make it possible to destroy them through police harassment, racial insensitivity, and provocative acts that lead to confrontation, resisting arrest, and, often, severe injury and death. In addition to police harassment, the court system daily condemns these young people to lives without a future. Labeled as demons before the trial and criminals before the sentence, many young people find themselves tried and convicted because of who they are and not what they have done. They literally find themselves guilty until they prove themselves innocent.

**"Riots are at bottom the language of the unheard."**
—**Martin Luther King Jr.**

**6. The violence of ignorance.**

This ignorance destroys a community's future by depriving it of (a) skills for employment and economic development; (b) accurate history that promotes self-esteem and truthful foundations about one's personality and people; and (c) the desire to learn as a value, with the excitement of expanding the mind in poetry, art, writing, science, and math. ■

**Questions:**

■ *This article outlines six ways violence is manifested. Are these manifestations apparent in your community? In your own life? Are there any you would add?*

■ *"Systemic racism" is racism based within social institutions, as opposed to racism solely at the personal level. It perpetuates policies that give unfair advantage to the white majority and penalizes minorities. Those carrying out the policy may be totally unaware of their participation in racism, because it is so ingrained. Can you think of examples of this in your community? How is this related to the violence of ignorance?*

# SAFE FOR YOUTH

*What your church can do.*

*by Yvonne Delk*

**1.** Dedicate your church as safe space for children and youth. Place a banner outside your church identifying it as safe space for children and young people.

**2.** Make a public statement identifying what your church is safe *for* and safe *from*. For instance:

| Safe From | Safe For |
|---|---|
| violence | tender and tough love |
| guns | affirmation |
| drugs | healing |
| hopelessness | strength |
| negative thinking | pride in identity, culture, history |
| estrangement and aloneness | community |
| demonic forces | honor and respect |
| homelessness | extended family |
| hunger | knowledge |
| unemployment | jobs |
| abuse | support |

**3.** Create after-school support programs for children and drop-in support centers for youth focused on self-awareness, personal efficacy, and personal responsibility.

**4.** Create a "rites of passage program" for children and youth that offers a program in African-American history, spirituality and values, vocation and economics, life and health, manhood and womanhood.

**5.** Establish tutorial centers after school in church facilities to help youngsters with learning disabilities. These tutors and mentors should be sought from within the church, fraterni-ties, sororities, the NAACP, the Urban League, and community and civic organizations.

**6.** Establish skills centers within the church to help youth with mathematics and reading deficiencies. Check with the local, state, and federal officials in terms of funding possibilities.

**7.** Make a concentrated effort to involve members of congregations, sororities, and fraternities, as well as other college students or leaders in the community, in conducting seminars in health, politics, test taking, nutrition, and African-American history.

**8.** Establish centers that provide counseling and support for chronic and addicted users of drugs.

**9.** Encourage individual members of your congregation to "adopt" a youngster who needs guidance and assistance. The principle of the "big brother" or "big sister" would apply in terms of serving as a role model and mentor.

**10.** Organize congregations to "adopt" public schools in the community. Members of the congregation would serve as advocates for the children and work closely with the school administrators on such issues as truancy, dropouts, disruptive behavior, expulsions, and school-community partnership.

Our children and our youth need a safe space. These suggestions offer an alternative to remaining idle while the statistics continue to climb. Take the initiative; stop the violence. ■

*YVONNE DELK is executive director of the Community Renewal Society (332 South Michigan, Chicago, IL 60604; (312) 423-4830).*

## Organizations:

■ **NAACP**, 4805 Mt. Hope Drive, Baltimore, MD 21215; (410) 358-8900.

■ **National Urban League**, 500 E. 62nd St., New York, NY 10021; (212) 310-9000.

## Questions:

■ *Historically the church has ministered to the troubled of society, which accounts for its designation as "sanctuary." Are churches today still seen as sanctuaries? How could you apply Delk's suggestions to make your church more inviting in this way? What are some other methods you would implement?*

■ *List important transitional times in the life of young people. What are some rites of passage that could be used to recognize these times of life change?*